Win a *Free* Classroom Set of Literature Connections!

FROM McDougal Littell

Join the growing community of educators who are using *Literature Connections* to teach the novels and plays they want to teach, each supplemented by additional readings bound together in one hardbound book.

Simply complete and return this postage-paid questionnaire card and you're automatically entered into the McDougal Littell drawing to win a free classroom set of the *Literature Connections* titles of your choice!

The Giver

Falen Angels — Walter Dean Myers
— Wilson Rawls
I, Juan de Pareja — Elizabeth Borton de Treviño
West with the Night — Beryl Markham
Johnny Tremain — Esther Forbes
The Adventures of Huckleberry Finn — Mark Twain
— Madeleine L'Engle
Yo, J... A Wrinkle in Time
Pygmalion — Elizabeth Borton de Treviño
— Bernard Shaw
— Charles Dickens
When Rain Clouds Gather — Bessie Head
The witch of Blackbird Pond — Elizabeth George Speare
A Raisin in the Sun — Lorraine Hansberry
Jane Eyre — Charlotte Brontë
— Nathaniel Hawthorne
A Midsummer Night's Dream
Hamlet — William Shakespeare
To Kill a Mockingbird: The Screenplay — William Shakespeare
— Horton Foote
A Tale of Two Cities — Charles Dickens
— Jack London
Things Fall Apart — Chinua Achebe
And the Earth Did Not Devour Him — Tomás Rivera
Llano en la tierra — Mildred D. Taylor
Tuck Everlasting — Natalie Babbitt
The House of Dies Drear — Virginia Hamilton
The Adventures of Huckleberry Finn — William Shakespeare
— Mark Twain
The Underdogs — Mariano Azuela
The Diary of Anne Frank — Frances Goodrich and Albert Hackett
— Tomás Rivera
— Sandra Benitez

LITERATURE CONNECTIONS

YES! Please enter me in the McDougal Littell Literature Connections drawing!

NAME_____

SCHOOL_____POSITION_____

SCHOOL ADDRESS_____CITY_____STATE_____ZIP_____

COUNTY_____SCHOOL DISTRICT/DIOCESE_____

COURSES TAUGHT_____

_____

EMAIL_____

WHAT NOVEL(S) OR PLAY(S) DO YOU TEACH?_____

ARE YOU USING LITERATURE CONNECTIONS IN YOUR CLASSES?   YES____ NO____

WOULD YOU LIKE TO BE INVOLVED IN FUTURE RESEARCH OR PRODUCT DEVELOPMENT? YES____ NO____

PHONE NUMBER: SCHOOL (_____)_____ HOME (_____)_____

FREE PERIOD_____

McDougal Littell

Information: 800-323-5435
International fax: 617-351-1132
Internet Address: http://www.mcdougallittell.com

P40166
1100.013

PC103

LITERATURE CONNECTIONS
SOURCEBOOK

Fallen Angels

and Related Readings

McDougal Littell
A HOUGHTON MIFFLIN COMPANY

Evanston, Illinois • Boston • Dallas

Links to *The Language of Literature*

If you are using *Fallen Angels* in conjunction with *The Language of Literature,* please note that thematic connections can be easily made between the novel and the following units:

- Grade 9, Unit 1: Live and Learn
- Grade 10, Unit 2: Reflecting on Society
- Grade 11, Unit 5: Conflict at Home and Abroad

Acknowledgments

Page 9: Excerpt from book review by Maria B. Salvadore in *School Library Journal*, June-July 1988. Copyright © by Cahners Publishing Company, a Division of Reed Elsevier Inc. Reprinted with permission from School Library Journal.

Page 9: Excerpt from book review by Ethel Hein in *The Horn Book Magazine*, July 1988. Reprinted by permission of The Horn Book, Inc., 11 Beacon Street, Suite 1000, Boston, MA 02108.

Page 10: Excerpt from book review by Mel Watkins in *The New York Times Book Review*, January 29, 1989. Copyright © 1989 by The New York Times Company. Reprinted by permission of The New York Times.

ISBN 0-395-78380-1

34567—MAL—03 02 01 00

Table of Contents

Parts of the SourceBook 2
Overview Chart. 3
Summaries of the LIterature 4
Customizing Instruction 5

Into the Literature: *Creating Context*

Fallen Angels 6
The Vietnam War. 6
The Language of War 6
Walter Dean Myers's Life 7
Myers on Myers 8
Critic's Corner. 9–10
Literary Concept: Theme. 11
Literary Concept: Characterization`. 12
Literary Concept: Conflict. 12
Motivating Activities. 13

Through the Literature: *Developing Understanding*

Fallen Angels Discussion Starters 14–17
Related Readings Discussion Starters 18–22
"The Things They Carried" 18
from *Dear America: Letters Home from Vietnam* 19
"In the Forest at Night" 19
"What Were They Like?" 20
"look at this)" 20
"The Spoils of War" 21
from "Ghosts in the Wall" 22
Reproducible Pages for Students 23
FYI: *Fallen Angels* 24–32
FYI: "The Things They Carried" 33
FYI: "In the Forest at Night" 34
FYI: "What Were They Like?" 35
FYI: "look at this)" 36
FYI: "The Spoils of War" 37
FYI: from "Ghosts in the Wall" 38
FYI: Glossary. 39–40
Strategic Reading 1–4. 41–44
Literary Concept 1–3 45–48
Vocabulary. 49

Beyond the Literature: *Synthesizing Ideas*

Culminating Writing Assignments. 50
Multimodal Activities 51–52
Cross-Curricular Projects 53–55
Suggestions for Assessment 56
Test 57–58
Test Answer Key. 59–60
Additional Resources 61–62

Parts of the SourceBook

- **Table of Contents**
- **Overview Chart**
- **Summaries of the Literature**
- **Customizing Instruction**

Into the Literature:
CREATING CONTEXT

- **Cultural/Historical/Author Background**
- **Critic's Corner** Excerpts from literary criticism about *Fallen Angels*
- **Literary Concepts**
- **Motivating Activities**

Through the Literature:
DEVELOPING UNDERSTANDING

- **Discussion Starters** Questions for the class to respond to orally after reading each section, including a Literary Concept question and a Writing Prompt
- **(FYI) FYI Pages for Students** Reproducible masters that offer students background, vocabulary help, and connections to the modern world
- **(FYI) Glossary** Reproducible two-page glossary of difficult words for student use from each section of *Fallen Angels*
- **Strategic Reading worksheets** Reproducible masters to help students keep track of the plot as they read (Literal and inferential reading)
- **Literary Concept worksheets** Reproducible masters to help students understand the use of literary elements (Critical reading)
- **Vocabulary worksheet** Reproducible master to help students learn essential vocabulary used in the novel

Beyond the Literature:
SYNTHESIZING IDEAS

- **Culminating Writing Assignments** Exploratory, research, and literary analysis topics for writing, covering both the main work and the related readings
- **Multimodal Activities** Suggestions for short-term projects, some of which are cross-curricular.
- **Cross-Curricular Projects** Suggestions for long-term, cross-curricular, cooperative-learning projects
- **Suggestions for Assessment**
- **Test, Answer Key** Essay and short-answer test on *Fallen Angels* and the related readings; answer key
- **Additional Resources** Additional readings for students (coded by difficulty level) and teachers, as well as bibliographic information about commercially available technology

Overview Chart

	PAGES FOR TEACHER'S USE	PAGES FOR STUDENT'S USE
Literature Connections	**SourceBook**	**Reproducible Pages**
Fallen Angels	Customizing Instruction, p. 5 Into the Literature: Creating Context, pp. 6–8 Critic's Corner, pp. 9–10 Literary Concepts: Theme, Characterization, Conflict, pp. 11–12 Motivating Activities, p. 13	**FYI, pp. 24–32** **Glossary, pp. 39–40** **Vocabulary worksheet, p. 49**
Fallen Angels Section 1, pp. 3–58	Discussion Starters, p. 14	**FYI, pp. 26–27, Glossary, p. 39** **Strategic Reading 1, p. 41** **Literary Concept 1, pp. 45–46**
Fallen Angels Section 2, pp. 59–122	Discussion Starters, p. 15	**FYI, p. 28, Glossary, p. 39** **Strategic Reading 2, p. 42** **Literary Concept 2, p. 47**
Fallen Angels Section 3, pp. 123–184	Discussion Starters, p. 16	**FYI, pp. 29–30, Glossary, p. 40** **Strategic Reading 3, p. 43** **Literary Concept 3, p. 48**
Fallen Angels Section 4, pp. 185–263	Discussion Starters, p. 17	**FYI, p. 31–32, Glossary, p. 40** **Strategic Reading 4, p. 44** **Literary Concept 1, pp. 45–46**
"The Things They Carried," pp. 269–291	Discussion Starter, p. 18	**FYI, p. 33**
from *Dear America: Letters Home from Vietnam*, pp. 292–296	Discussion Starters, p. 19	
"In the Forest at Night," pp. 297–300	Discussion Starters, p. 19	**FYI, p. 34**
"What Were They Like?," pp. 301–302	Discussion Starters, p. 20	**FYI, p. 35**
"look at this)" p. 303	Discussion Starters, p. 20	**FYI, p. 36**
"The Spoils of War," pp. 304–308	Discussion Starters, p. 21	**FYI, p. 37**
from "Ghosts in the Wall," pp. 309–313	Discussion Starters, p. 22	**FYI, p. 38**
	Culminating Writing Assignments, p. 50 Multimodal Activities, pp. 47–48 Cross-Curricular Projects, pp. 53–55 Suggestions for Assessment, p. 56 Test, Answer Key, pp. 57–60 Additional Resources, pp. 61–62	

Additional writing support for students can be found in the **Writing Coach.**

Fallen Angels
by Walter Dean Myers

In this award-winning novel Myers presents the myriad experiences of a group of men who come of age during the Vietnam War. Richie Perry, the novel's protagonist and narrator, enlists in the army mainly to escape his problems—an alcoholic mother, a lack of opportunity in Harlem, and uncertainty about his future. He finds himself in the middle of a war that is more confusing and traumatic than the life he fled. Eventually, after being wounded in action, Perry and his friend Peewee Gates return to "the World."

RELATED READINGS

The Things They Carried
by Tim O'Brien

One of a series of interconnected short stories by award-winning author and Vietnam veteran Tim O'Brien, this story examines the burdens—both physical and emotional—that a platoon of soldiers in Vietnam must bear.

from Dear America: Letters Home from Vietnam
by George Olsen

In this letter home to the United States, a soldier in Vietnam discusses why he is fighting in a faraway country.

In the Forest at Night
by Duc Thanh, translated by Thanh T. Nguyen and Bruce Weigl

The human face of the enemy is revealed in this poem written by a North Vietnamese soldier.

What Were They Like?
by Denise Levertov

Written by a prominent anti-war protester, this poem makes a powerful statement against the war by asking what Vietnam was like before the conflict began.

look at this)
by E. E. Cummings

This poem, written after World War I, confronts the stark reality of death in wartime.

The Spoils of War
by Lynne Sharon Schwartz

The author gives a vivid portrait of the emotional scars the war has left on a Vietnam veteran who is studying in her class.

from Ghosts in the Wall
by Kris Hardin

This excerpt from an essay describes the planning and building of the Vietnam Veterans Memorial, and it explores the role the memorial has played in helping the United States come to terms with the war.

Customizing Instruction

Less Proficient Readers

- Read aloud key chapters from the novel. As students follow along in their books, have them keep a log of the characters' names, including military ranks and brief descriptions.

- Have small groups of students read aloud passages from the novel that feature conversations among Perry and other members of his squad. Each character's dialogue can be read aloud by a different student.

- To help with literal comprehension of the plot and characters, reproduce and have students use **Strategic Reading 1–4** worksheets, pages 41–44, as they read.

Students Acquiring English

- If any students are familiar with Southeast Asian culture—especially Vietnamese culture—have them share their knowledge with the class. For example, these students might discuss the holiday of Tet— the lunar new year—celebrated not only in the countries of Southeast Asia but also in the United States by Vietnamese Americans.

- Some students may come from countries that have suffered through war in recent years. If you feel your classroom situation is appropriate, have these students discuss the impact of life in a war-torn country, drawing on their own recollections or those of family members.

- Bring in books containing photographs of the Vietnam War. As students examine the pictures, guide them to draw conclusions about the historical and cultural setting of the novel.

- If appropriate, use the suggestions for Less Proficient Readers listed above.

Gifted and Talented Students

- Share the **Critic's Corner** literary reviews with students and encourage them to find other critical essays on Walter Dean Myers's work. Have them write an opinion essay addressing one of the issues raised in the reviews.

- Have students create a time line of key events in U.S. history from the beginning of 1967 through the end of 1968. As they read *Fallen Angels,* they can add important fictional events from the novel to the time line. They might share their findings in an oral report to the class.

1967   1968   1969

Fallen Angels

In *Fallen Angels*, Myers presents the myriad experiences of a group of young soldiers who come of age during the Vietnam War. Critics have compared this 1988 novel with an array of post-Vietnam books and with other war literature, including Stephen Crane's classic *The Red Badge of Courage*.

Like Crane, Myers never had actual combat experience. He did enlist in the army, but his service ended a decade before the time period of the novel—1967 to 1968. However, Myers did not escape the shattering experience of coping with violent death during the Vietnam War. His younger brother, Thomas Myers, served—and was killed—in Vietnam.

The Vietnam War

U.S. involvement in Vietnam began long before U.S. troops were in combat. After World War II, the French fought to regain control of Vietnam, which had been part of their colony French Indochina since the late 1800s. When the communist leader Ho Chi Minh organized a revolt in northern Vietnam, the United States aided France in the war that ensued. The war ended in 1954, when Vietnam was temporarily divided into two parts. Ho Chi Minh established a communist government in North Vietnam, and the territory in the south became the Republic of Vietnam.

In 1957, a group of South Vietnamese communists, the Vietcong, rebelled against the South Vietnamese government. In 1964, after President Johnson convinced Congress that the Communists had attacked a U.S. warship, Congress granted him the power to escalate American military involvement. In 1965 President Johnson authorized the bombing of Vietnam, and the first U.S ground troops arrived. *Fallen Angels* begins in late 1967 and ends shortly after the Tet Offensive of January 1968, when the Vietcong launched a major attack on about 100 towns and cities. The Vietnam War—the longest and perhaps the most divisive war in American history—ended in 1975.

The Language of War

Hundreds of terms—military jargon, acronyms, and slang expressions—entered the English language during the Vietnam War. The characters in *Fallen Angels* learn to speak and understand much of the lingo. For example, they refer to a powerful machine gun as "the M-60," "the sixty," and "the pig." However, they show confusion at certain military terms such as "interdiction patrol," "maximizing destruction," and "pacification," whose true meanings they find difficult to discern. The characters also use the foul language typically spoken by soldiers at war. Their swearing lends a realism to the novel and is authentic to its historical setting.

Note: This novel depicts events that some readers may find disturbing and includes language that some may find objectionable.

Myers's Life

1937	Born on August 12 in Martinsburg, West Virginia.
1940	At the age of three, moves to Harlem with his foster parents, Herbert and Florence Dean.
1941	Florence Dean teaches four-year-old Myers to read.
1955–58	Serves in the United States Army.
1966–1969	Works as an employment supervisor at the New York State Department of Labor in Brooklyn.
1968	Wins the Council on Interracial Books for Children Award for his manuscript of *Where Does the Day Go?Where Does the Day Go?*
	Myers's brother, Thomas Wayne "Sonny" Myers, is killed in the Vietnam War.
1970–77	Works as a senior trade editor at Bobbs-Merrill publishing company.
1973	Marries Constance Brendel, his second wife.
1974–75	Teaches creative writing and history classes part-time.
1977	Begins to earn his living as a full-time writer.
1980	Wins the Coretta Scott King Award for his book, *The Young Landlords*.
1988	Publishes *Fallen Angels*, which receives rave reviews.
1989	*Fallen Angels* wins the Coretta Scott King Award.
1993	Publishes *The Glory Field*, which wins numerous awards.

Myers on Myers

On his childhood in Harlem—

"I found Harlem a marvel, an exotic land with an inexhaustible supply of delights and surprises. . . . I loved Harlem. . . . The tarred streets, the fire escapes upon which we sought relief from the heat, two-sewer stickball, Chinese handball; this was the stuff of dreams. . . . Yet this was not the Harlem I saw portrayed in books. . . . That space of earth was no ghetto, it was home."

FROM *SOMETHING ABOUT THE AUTHOR*, VOLUME 41

On joining the army—

"I read the poems of Rupert Brooke and suddenly it came to me what I had to do. I would hie myself off to some far-off battlefield and get killed. There, where I fell, would be a little piece of Harlem. At 17, I joined the army. I didn't tell my parents I joined until the morning I left. . . . I spent most of my time in the service playing basketball. I also learned several efficient ways of killing human beings. And with images from poets like Byron and Brooke and Spender loosely in my mind, I was ready to do battle with anyone."

FROM *SOMETHING ABOUT THE AUTHOR AUTOBIOGRAPHY SERIES*, VOLUME 2

On images of African Americans in the media—

"[As an editor] I was . . . gaining an awareness of the Black image in literature, film, and television. The image was disturbing. Blacks were portrayed as nonserious people. . . . Remembering my own childhood, I realized what an effect that had on the Black child."

FROM *SOMETHING ABOUT THE AUTHOR AUTOBIOGRAPHY SERIES*, VOLUME 2

On subjects for writing—

"As a writer there are many issues I would like to tackle. I am interested in loneliness, in our attempts to escape reality. . . . I am interested in how we deal with each other . . . and the reasons we often reject each other. . . . As a Black writer I want to talk about my people. . . . I want to tell Black children about their humanity and their history . . ."

FROM *SOMETHING ABOUT THE AUTHOR AUTOBIOGRAPHY SERIES*, VOLUME 2

On the legacy of writing—

"I try not to make too much of my writing. My grandfather told stories, my father told stories, and that is what I do. Because I have published mine does not make me better than those who have gone before me."

FROM *SOMETHING ABOUT THE AUTHOR AUTOBIOGRAPHY SERIES*, VOLUME 2

Critic's Corner

Maria B. Salvadore

Salvadore, Maria B., Rev. of *Fallen Angels*, by Walter Dean Myers, *School Library Journal* June-July 1988: 118

A riveting account of the Vietnam War from the perspective of a young black soldier [Richie Perry]. . . . His first-person narrative provides an immediacy to the events and characters revealed. His experiences become the readers' experiences, as do his fears and his insight about war, any war. "We spent another day lying around. It seemed to be what war was about. Hours of boredom, seconds of terror." . . . This is a compelling, graphic, necessarily gruesome novel. It neither condemns nor glorifies the war, but certainly causes readers to think about the events. Other difficult issues, such as race and the condition of Vietnamese people, are sensitively and realistically incorporated into the novel. The soldiers' language is raw, but appropriate to the characters.

Ethel L. Heins

Heins, Ethel L., Rev. of *Fallen Angels*, by Walter Dean Myers, *Horn Book* July-August 1988: 503

Adolescents have certainly been followers of the recent truth-telling films about the Vietnam War, but there remains a dearth of young adult fiction on the subject. Yet literature written with authenticity and honesty may well imprint itself on the human mind in ways that even the strongest films, with their fleeting images, cannot duplicate. Fortunately, the author of the new novel [*Fallen Angels*] is a writer of skill, maturity, and judgment. . . . Except for occasional outbursts, the narration is remarkably direct and understated, and the dialogue, with morbid humor sometimes adding comic relief, is steeped in natural vulgarity, without which verisimilitude would be unthinkable. In fact, the foul talk, which serves as the story's linguistic setting, is not nearly as obscene as some of the events. With its intensity and vividness in depicting a young soldier amid the chaos and the carnage of war, the novel recalls Stephen Crane's *The Red Badge of Courage*.

Critic's Corner

Mel Watkins

Watkins, Mel, Rev. of *Fallen Angels*, by Walter Dean Myers, *The New York Times Book Review* 22 Jan. 1989: 29

"Where the hell is your pride, soldier?" an Army captain asks one of his men in this fictional trek through the trenches of the Vietnamese conflict in the late 1960s. And the response—"In Chicago, sir. Can I go get it?"—more or less sets the tone for Walter Myers's graphic tale of combat soldiers in our most unpopular war.

The story is told through the eyes of Richard Perry, a Harlem teenager who volunteers for the services when his dreams of attending college are frustrated and he becomes disenchanted with street life. In a sense, the novel is just as much about Perry's coming of age as it is about the Vietnam War. Perry's experience in Vietnam—his baptism in the violence, confusion, and moral havoc—is the crucible that tests and determines his passage to manhood.

Equally important to his growth are the many people he encounters. Although there are some stock battlefield characters here—the tough sergeant; the weak, sensitive recruit; the hardened no-nonsense veteran officer—Mr. Myers has also peopled his novel with some refreshing, original characters. Foremost among them is Peewee Gates, a black soldier from Chicago, whose humor and unique view of life act as a counterpoint to the grim depiction of war's reality. . . . Mr. Myers . . . [allows] his main characters to emerge as interesting, complex people, rather than just stereotypical soldiers. . . .

Mr. Myers also touches on many of the ironies and vagaries peculiar to the Vietnam conflict: the ever-present problem of determining which Vietnamese are the enemy; the racial tension growing in part from the assignment of black troops to the most hazardous positions; the endless conflict between the United States Army and the South Vietnamese; the political overtones of the war; and the nagging question of why we were there. Wisely, the story never becomes a platform for discussing these issues; they arise out of the characters' interaction with one another and from the day-to-day routine of the GI's.

Fallen Angels is a candid young adult novel that engages the Vietnam experience squarely. It deals with violence and death as well as compassion and love. . . . It is a tale that is as thought-provoking as it is entertaining, touching, and, on occasion, humorous.

Literary Concept
THEME

The **theme** of a literary work is a perception about life or human nature that the writer presents to the reader. *Fallen Angels* explores issues surrounding the nature of war and the experience of coming of age. For example, in Chapter 14, Richie Perry reflects on his newfound maturity and the ordeal of combat:

> I had come into the army at seventeen, and I remembered who I was, and who I was had been a kid. The war hadn't meant anything to me then, maybe because I had never gone through anything like it before. All I had thought about combat was that I would never die, that our side would win, and that we would all go home somehow satisfied. And now all the dying around me, and all the killing, was making me look at myself again, hoping to find something more than the kid I was. (p. 158)

Such rites of passage run throughout *Fallen Angels*. Below are some of the specific issues in the novel that flesh out Myers's treatment of the theme of war and its impact:

- Young soldiers engaged in combat typically undergo a personal transformation—a passage from youth to maturity, from innocence to experience.
- Warfare often forces soldiers to reconsider their traditional notions of right and wrong.
- The conditions of war show the true nature of heroism.
- Friendships and bonds are often intensified among people who share constant danger and the threat of sudden death.
- War brings out extremes of behavior—not only courage, loyalty, and sacrifice but also brutality, prejudice, and arrogance.
- War is chaotic: Soldiers often find it difficult to make sense of or find meaning in combat.
- The experiences of war may leave long-lasting emotional scars on soldiers, civilians, and nations.

Presentation Suggestions Help students discover these and other themes as they read. If you wish to have students discuss the major themes prior to reading the novel, you may use **Literary Concept 1,** pages 45–46, as a prereading activity. You might stop students at the end of each section of the novel and ask which thematic statements are suggested by the events or characters.

Literary Concept
CHARACTERIZATION

Walter Dean Myers has a reputation for creating authentic characters. The vivid portrayal of characters in *Fallen Angels* reinforces Myers's powerful theme about the impact of war. The methods that a writer uses to develop characters are known as characterization. Here are four basic methods of **characterization** in fiction:

- description of a character's physical appearance
- a character's speech, thoughts, feelings, and actions
- the speech, thoughts, feelings, and actions of other characters in relation to a character
- direct comments about a character's nature

Presentation Suggestions   As students read, encourage them to consider how they learn about the different characters in the novel. **Literary Concept 2,** page 47, can be used to further explore the concept of characterization.

Literary Concept
CONFLICT

In William Faulkner's acceptance speech for the Nobel Prize in literature in 1950, he expressed this concern: "[T]he young man or woman writing today has forgotten the problems of the human heart in conflict with itself. . . . He [or she] must learn them again." In *Fallen Angels*, Myers has written about these internal conflicts—the struggles that occur within "the heart" of a character. For example, throughout the novel Richie Perry struggles with the opposing forces of right and wrong as a soldier whose job is "killing the enemy."

Fallen Angels is also filled with external conflicts involving characters pitted against outside forces, such as nature, physical obstacles, or other characters. The most obvious external conflict is between the soldiers and the enemy they are fighting. However, Perry and the members of his squad also contend with the heat, humidity, and unfamiliar terrain of Vietnam. Clashes also sometimes occur between characters, such as Johnson and Walowick.

Presentation Suggestions   You may wish to remind students that the **conflict** in a literary work means the struggle between two opposing forces. As students read, encourage them to cite examples of both internal conflicts and external conflicts in the novel. **Literary Concept 3,** page 48, can be used to help them explore these literary concepts.

Motivating Activities

1. **Brainstorming List** Direct students to list popular images of warfare and soldiers as portrayed in movies, television shows, novels, comic books, video games, and so on.

2. **Word Web** Have students write the word Vietnam, and then create a word web of words and phrases they associate with this country, its culture, and history.

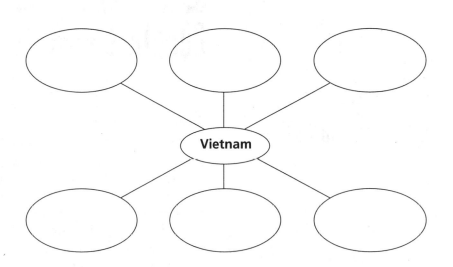

3. **Tapping Prior Knowledge: The Vietnam War** Ask students to work together as a class or in small groups to share what they know about the Vietnam War. Encourage students to think about stories they may have heard from family members who remember the Vietnam War, as well as documentaries and movies they have seen. Record facts and impressions on the board.

4. **Linking to Today: Military Conflicts** Encourage students to name any military conflicts they can think of that have occurred during their own lifetimes—for example, the Gulf War, or the war in Bosnia. Help them explore their views on issues such as the reasons countries go to war, the role technology plays in modern warfare, and the effects of war on both soldiers and civilians. Encourage students to search newspapers and magazines for recent accounts of military conflicts.

5. **Quickwrite: Staying Alive** Have students write about how they think they might react in a life-or-death situation, such as a war or a natural disaster. Encourage them to explore possible reactions. For example, would they panic or freeze? take foolish risks? show grace under pressure? sacrifice their lives to save others?

6. **FYI Background** Reproduce and distribute to students the FYI pages that give background information on *Fallen Angels* and the Vietnam War (pages 24–25). You might at this time reproduce and distribute all the FYI pages for the novel for students to refer to as they read.

BEFORE READING

You might want to distribute

(FYI) *pp. 26–27, Glossary, p. 39*
- *Strategic Reading 1, p. 41*
- *Literary Concept 1, pp. 45–46*

Fallen Angels

SECTION 1
Chapters 1–5

AFTER READING

Discussion Starters

1. How would you respond to Perry's concluding remark (Chapter 5)?
2. What is your opinion of Perry at this point in the novel?
3. **Making Connections** If you were in Richie Perry's situation after graduating high school, would you have enlisted in the armed forces? Why or why not?
4. How would you account for the strong bonds that develop among the African-American soldiers?
5. Why does Perry go out on patrol despite his medical profile? Give at least two reasons and support them with details from the novel.

> ### CONSIDER
>
> ✓ officers' responses to Perry's early questions about his medical profile
>
> ✓ Perry's discussion with Lieutenant Carroll about his medical profile
>
> ✓ Peewee's advice after Perry's discussion with Lieutenant Carroll

6. **Literary Concept: Symbol** A symbol is a person, a place, an object, or an action that stands for something beyond itself. In his prayer for Jenkins, Lieutenant Carroll describes soldiers as "angel warriors." What do you think angels symbolize in this description?
7. What incidents described in this section of the novel could have occurred to a young soldier entering any war? What incidents could have only happened in Vietnam during the 1960s? Explain and give examples.

Writing Prompt

Imagine you are a new recruit in Perry's squad going out on your first patrol. Write a **letter** to a friend or family member at home about your experiences.

BEFORE READING

You might want to distribute

(FYI) *p. 28, Glossary, p. 39*

• *Strategic Reading 2, p. 42*

• *Literary Concept 2, p. 47*

SECTION 2

Chapters 6–11

AFTER READING

Discussion Starters

1. What thoughts did you have after reading the description of Lieutenant Carroll's face on the television screen?

2. Compare and contrast Lieutenant Carroll's, Lobel's, and Perry's political and personal reasons for fighting the war.

> ### CONSIDER
>
> ✓ their responses during the television interview
>
> ✓ their comments about their upbringings and family relationships before they enlisted

2. **Literary Concept: Characterization** Why do you think Perry wants to be liked by the Vietnamese?

3. After Lieutenant Carroll dies, Perry says, "The war was different now" (p. 115). Why do you think this death has changed Perry's view of the war?

4. How would you describe the ways that Perry and his squad cope with the day-to-day stress caused by the war?

> ### CONSIDER
>
> ✓ their relationships with one another
>
> ✓ the activities they pursue
>
> ✓ the topics they discuss
>
> ✓ their reactions to Lieutenant Carroll's death

5. Compare and contrast Perry's relationship with his brother Kenny to your own relationship with a brother, sister, or cousin.

6. **Literary Concept: Theme** Cite incidents from this section of the novel that support Perry's description of what war is about: "Hours of boredom. Seconds of terror" (p. 111).

7. **Making Connections** What are some historic moments or events that you have viewed on television? Do you think that the television coverage presented an objective account of history in the making? Explain your answer.

Writing Prompt

Write an **obituary** for Lieutenant Carroll describing his special qualities.

SECTION 3

Chapters 12–16

AFTER READING

Discussion Starters

1. What word best describes Perry's state of mind as he gets ready to rejoin his unit after his release from the hospital?

2. On a scale of 1 to 10, rate the leadership skills of both Sergeant Simpson and Lieutenant Gearhart. Support your ratings with evidence from the text.

CONSIDER

✓ how each officer treats the men in his command

✓ how each officer performs in battle

3. How would you answer Johnson's question to Perry, "What you think about them protesters?" (p. 125).

4. Based on your reading, what do you consider to be the strengths and weaknesses of the American soldiers and the Vietcong soldiers? Support your answer with evidence from the novel.

5. **Literary Concept: Internal Conflict** An internal conflict is a struggle between opposing forces within a character. What internal conflicts plague Perry as he decides on the content of his letters to his brother Kenny?

CONSIDER

✓ letters that Perry composes but never sends

✓ experiences and insights that are omitted in the letters

6. **Making Connections** While in Vietnam, Perry's thoughts often drift back to Harlem. Compare and contrast Perry's feelings for Harlem with your feelings for the place where you grew up.

Writing Prompt

Perry has a terrifying dream about the Vietcong he shot. Write a **description** of a nightmare, real or imagined, involving a memory that haunts you.

SECTION 4

Chapters 17—23

AFTER READING

Discussion Starters

1. What are your main concerns for Perry as he returns to "the World"?

2. What values and beliefs do you think guide Sergeant Dongan's actions?

CONSIDER

- ✓ Perry's observations about Dongan's upbringing
- ✓ Dongan's comments about his military experiences during the Korean War
- ✓ Johnson's, Peewee's, Monaco's, and Perry's remarks about Dongan's prejudice

3. Why do you think that Perry finds General Westmoreland's request to "maximize destruction of the enemy" so disturbing?

4. Perry remarks, "We [Monaco, Peewee, and Perry] had tasted what it was like being dead. . . . We would have to learn to be alive again" (p. 259). What steps do you think they will have to take to regain their sense of being alive?

5. Do you think that Perry and Peewee's friendship will weaken or grow stronger after their return to the United States?

CONSIDER

- ✓ what makes their friendship special
- ✓ what circumstances await them at home
- ✓ reasons they might have for maintaining or not maintaining their relationship

6. What do you think is the most important social or political issue raised in the novel's final section? Support your answer with examples from the text.

7. **Making Connections** Perry says, "You know, to a kid if you kill somebody and the somebody is supposed to be a bad guy, you're a hero" (p. 228). How do you think most young people define heroism? Compare and contrast your definition with Perry's.

8. **Literary Concept: Theme** How would you explain the main message that Walter Dean Myers conveys about the war in Vietnam?

9. Compare Perry's feelings about coming home alive to those of other survivors of great catastrophes—plane crashes, natural disasters, and so on. What emotions do you think survivors of such extreme situations share?

Writing Prompt

Write a **scene** from a one-act play featuring Perry's reunion with his mother and brother.

You might want to distribute

FYI *p. 33*

RELATED READINGS

The Things They Carried

AFTER READING

Discussion Starters

1. What image lingers in your mind after reading this story?

2. How would you describe Lieutenant Cross's relationship with Martha?

3. Do you think that Lieutenant Cross is responsible in any way for Ted Lavender's death? Why or why not?

4. Do you think Lieutenant Cross will achieve the new goals he has set for himself? Why or why not?

5. What do you think is the significance of the title of this story?

6. **Literary Concept: Style** What effect do you think the author achieves by the repetition of the phrase "they carried"?

7. Would you describe this story as antiwar, pro-war, or neither? Support your answer with details from the story.

8. In *Fallen Angels*, Perry remarks, "Having people care about you was probably the only thing that made any of it [the war] right. Having them not care about you made your life wrong" (pp. 169–170). Do you think Lieutenant Cross would agree with this statement? Why or why not?

Writing Prompt

Imagine you are a soldier under Lieutenant Cross's command in Vietnam. Write a detailed **list** of the personal items you would carry in your backpack. Include the reasons for carrying these items, such as their sentimental value, usefulness, and so on.

from Dear America: Letters Home from Vietnam

Discussion Starters

1. What is your impression of George Olsen?
2. Why do you think Olsen believes that writing this letter will make him feel better?
3. Do you think that Olsen fairly judges the Amish, a Protestant group that opposes war for religious reasons? Why or why not?
4. Do you think Olsen is making a valid point in his story about wolves and sheep? Explain your opinion.
5. Compare and contrast the moral codes—the standards of right and wrong—that George Olsen and Richie Perry live by during wartime.

Writing Prompt

Imagine Olsen's letter was written to you. Write a **letter** in response.

BEFORE READING

You might want to distribute

(FYI) *p. 34*

In the Forest at Night

Discussion Starters

1. Did this poem change your attitude toward the "enemy" U.S. soldiers fought in Vietnam? Explain your answer.

   > **CONSIDER**
   > - ✓ the hardships he endures
   > - ✓ his statement that he is "the son of the Vietnamese" (line 9)
   > - ✓ his mention of his mother (stanza 4)
   > - ✓ the last stanza

2. What is your impression of the speaker of this poem?
3. How universal do you think the speaker's sentiments are about war?
4. Compare and contrast the feelings that the speaker of the poem expresses about his mother with the emotions Richie Perry conveys about his mother.

Writing Prompt

Write a **letter to the editor** in which you express your own views about war and patriotism.

You might want to distribute

(FYI) *p. 35*

What Were They Like?

Discussion Starters

1. What do you think is the most disturbing image in the poem? the most beautiful image? Give reasons for your choices.
2. Why do you think the poet chose a question-and-answer format for the poem?
3. **Literary Concept: Tone** How would you describe the tone of this poem?

> ### CONSIDER
>
> ✓ the definition of tone as the attitude a writer takes toward a subject
> ✓ such phrases as "laughter is bitter to the burned mouth" (line 16)

4. In Chapter 20 of *Fallen Angels*, Peewee asks Perry two questions about the Vietcong: "What they names?" and "What they like to eat?" Because Perry doesn't know the answers, Peewee tells him, "See, they ain't people to you yet" (p. 228). How do you think the speaker in the second half of this poem would respond to Peewee's questions and statement?

Writing Prompt

Think about people you have read about in the news who are victims of violent acts, such as military conflicts, terrorism, or street crimes. Write a **character sketch** in which you give a human face to one of these victims.

You might want to distribute

(FYI) *p. 36*

look at this]

Discussion Starters

1. Describe the scene that comes to mind as you read this poem.
2. What do you think was the speaker's relationship with the dead soldier?
3. Do you agree with what the speaker is saying about the casualties of war?
4. What event in *Fallen Angels* reminds you most of the incident described in this poem? Explain your answer.

Writing Prompt

Write a **review** of this poem, looking at how the poet's style and use of imagery help to establish the theme.

You might want to distribute
(FYI) *p. 37*

The Spoils of War

AFTER READING

Discussion Starters

1. Do you agree with the point made at the end of this article? Explain your opinion.

2. How would you describe the Vietnam veteran in this article?

3. Did this article change your image of Vietnam veterans? Why or why not?

4. Think about the student-teacher relationship between the Vietnam veteran and Lynne Sharon Schwartz, as described in this article, and the relationship in *Fallen Angels* between Richie Perry and Ms. Liebow, his high school English teacher. What are the similarities and differences?

5. **Making Connections** Describe an occasion on which you, or someone you know, misjudged a person based on his or her appearance or manner.

Writing Prompt

The student profiled in "The Spoils of War" wrote a paper on the meaning of "the horror" in Joseph Conrad's short novel *Heart of Darkness*. Write a brief **essay** explaining the meaning of the word *horror* based on a story you have read, a movie you have seen, or an event in history you know about.

from Ghosts in the Wall

Discussion Starters

1. What was your reaction to the gestures of remembrance described at the end of this article?

2. Why do you think Jan Scruggs wanted private donations, rather than government funds, to pay for building a Vietnam memorial?

3. One of the rules governing the competition for the memorial was that the design could make no political statements about the war. Do you think Richie Perry and other members of his squad would consider this rule fair or unfair? Explain your answer.

4. Do you agree with Maya Lin's view that "soldiers cannot be seen as individuals when they fight or when they die"? Support your answer with reasons.

5. In preparation for her proposal, Maya Lin read about how people in different places around the world deal with grief. What are some ways that people from your cultural background mourn and remember the dead?

6. Based on this article, how would you describe the healing process that the U.S. underwent following the Vietnam War?

Writing Prompt

Imagine you are a news reporter covering the building of the Vietnam Veterans Memorial. Write a list of **interview questions** that you would ask either Jan Scruggs or Maya Lin.

These pages for the students give background, explain references, help with vocabulary words, and help students connect the contemporary world with the world of *Fallen Angels*. You can reproduce them and allow students to read them before or while they are reading the works in *Literature Connections*.

Table of Contents

Background 24–25

Section 1: Chapters 1–5 26–27

Section 2: Chapters 6–11 28

Section 3: Chapters 12–16 29–30

Section 4: Chapters 17–23 31–32

"The Things They Carried" 33

"In the Forest at Night" 34

"What Were They Like?" 35

"look at this)" 36

"The Spoils of War" 37

from "Ghosts in the Wall" 38

Glossary 39–40

Fallen Angels

BACKGROUND

The Vietnam War

1945 Ho Chi Minh proclaims Democratic Republic of Vietnam.

1950 First U.S. military aid given to the French.

1954 French defeated at Dien Bien Phu; Vietnam is temporarily divided at the 17th Parallel (the DMZ).

1961 President Kennedy increases number of military advisers to Vietnam. The first GI is killed.

1965 First Marines arrive in Vietnam; bombing of North Vietnam begins.

1968 Communists launch Tet offensive; Paris peace talks begin.

1969 President Nixon orders staged withdrawal of American troops.

1970 U.S. troops enter Cambodia to destroy Communist bases.

1972 Last U.S. ground combat troops leave Vietnam.

1973 Cease-fire in Vietnam after truce agreement signed in Paris. Last U.S. military personnel leave.

1975 Saigon falls to the North Vietnamese and is renamed Ho Chi Minh City.

DMZ Lingo

The map shows the DMZ—the demilitarized zone—which divided North and South Vietnam at the 17th parallel. Here are some slang expressions soldiers used in referring to the DMZ.

- D and the Z
- Dead Man's Zone
- Dead Marine's Zone
- the D
- Ultra Militarized Zone

The Land of Two Rice Baskets

Vietnam forms an S-shaped curve winding along the coastline of Southeast Asia. The Vietnamese sometimes describe the contours of their country as resembling two rice baskets dangling from opposite ends of a farmer's bamboo pole. The river deltas in North Vietnam and South Vietnam each form a "basket," and the narrow strip of land between them forms the "pole." The geography of Vietnam consists of fertile agricultural areas, particularly around the river deltas; rugged mountainous regions; and lush tropical jungles.

Fallen Angels (continued)

BACKGROUND

The Key Players—A Who's Who

Lyndon B. Johnson President of the United States from 1963 to 1969. His "guns and butter" administration was committed to winning two wars: the war in Southeast Asia and the War on Poverty at home.

General William C. Westmoreland American military commander in South Vietnam from 1965 to 1968. In his memoir, *A Soldier Reports,* he described the U.S. soldiers in Vietnam as "the finest military force . . . ever assembled."

Ho Chi Minh Vietnamese communist leader. His name means "He Who Enlightens" or "Bringer of Light."

General Vo Nguyen Giap Commander of Ho Chi Minh's military forces. The French nicknamed him the "snow-covered volcano" because his cold, aloof manner masked his seething temper.

The Elephant and the Tiger

In 1946 a war broke out between the French, who had ruled Vietnam since the late 1800s as part of their colony known as French Indochina, and the Vietminh, an organization of communists and other nationalists under the leadership of Ho Chi Minh. Before the war began, Ho Chi Minh compared the impending conflict to the struggle between an elephant (the French) and a tiger (the Vietminh):

> **"If the tiger ever stands still, the elephant will crush him with his mighty tusks. But the tiger will not stand still. He will leap upon the back of the elephant, tearing huge chunks from his side, and then he will leap back into the dark jungle. And slowly the elephant will bleed to death. Such will be the war in Indochina."**

Ho Chi Minh's retelling of this ancient Vietnamese folk tale was prophetic. The Vietnamese finally defeated the French in 1954 and later exhausted the power and strength of another elephant—the United States. As George Ball, Undersecretary of State under President Lyndon Johnson, remarked about U.S. military involvement in Vietnam, "Once on the tiger's back, we cannot be sure of picking the place to dismount."

Chain of Command

Rank

GENERAL
COLONEL
MAJOR
CAPTAIN
LIEUTENANT
SERGEANT
CORPORAL

Military Unit

FIELD ARMY
REGIMENT
BATTALION
COMPANY
PLATOON
SQUAD

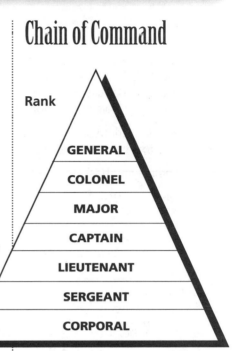

In His Own Image

Walter Dean Myers and the character he invented, Richie Perry, share some striking similarities. Here are some things they have in common:

- grew up in Harlem and felt a deep connection to this place

- enjoyed playing basketball

- attended Stuyvesant High School

- had an encouraging high school English teacher named Liebow

- had early aspirations to become a writer

- enlisted in the army at age 17 because college was unaffordable

Harlem

Harlem pervades many of Walter Dean Myers's novels—even *Fallen Angels*, set far away in Vietnam. Richie Perry may be fighting in Vietnam, but his daydreams often take him back to Harlem, his hometown. Through Perry's eyes, the reader catches glimpses of the people he knows from this New York City neighborhood, as well as its parks, playgrounds, schools, and theaters.

Harlem is a mainly African-American community with a rich history. Many cultural leaders, sports heroes, musicians, and writers have lived there, including Langston Hughes. In fact, Hughes once chased Myers's brother down the block for tossing a candy wrapper in his garden.

How Old?

Richie Perry enlists in the army at the age of 17. The average age of a GI in Vietnam was just 19 years old—7 years younger than the average age of GI's fighting in World War II.

Chapter 2

Naming the Enemy

The name *Vietcong* was first used in 1954 to refer to the Vietnamese communists, the rebel group in South Vietnam. Later the U.S. military used "VC" as an abbreviation for Vietcong. However, soldiers were instructed to avoid using letters when communicating messages on the radio because sounds might be difficult to distinguish during transmission. Instead, soldiers learned to substitute code words for letters of the alphabet. The code words for VC were "Victor Charlie." Soldiers started referring to the enemy as simply "Charlie." Among the other nicknames they used were Victor, Chas, Chuck, Charles, and Mr. Charles.

Chapter 1

Lights! Cameras! Vietnam!

Lobel fantasizes about stopping "this silly war and . . . making the movies right away" (p. 41) and casting the Vietcong in Hollywood's Vietnam War films. The Vietnam War did, of course, reach the silver screen. Movie images of soldiers and Vietnam veterans have ranged from downtrodden infantrymen and ruthless killers in combat films to comic-book heroes and trigger-happy cops in action-adventure films. Academy Award-winning films such as *The Deer Hunter* and *Platoon* have shown a more realistic picture of the war and its aftermath.

Some of these Vietnam War films were very different from traditional war movies. Watching them, audiences often had trouble distinguishing between the "good guys" and the "bad guys." This portrayal of the war was a reflection of the nation's uncertainty about the conflict: the Vietnam War was not World War II—"the good war," the war we won.

Chapter 4

LITERARY CONCEPT
Symbol

The word *angel* conjures up familiar images of heavenly winged creatures. As well as having religious significance for many people, such images have become a part of our general culture.

Angels are also commonly used as a symbol—a person, a place, an object, or an activity that stands for something beyond itself. As a symbol, angels may represent protection, innocence, and purity. In literature, the context in which a symbol is used will help you to determine what the symbol represents. Lieutenant Carroll refers to Jenkins and other soldiers killed in action as "angel warriors that fall." The fact that Myers has titled his novel *Fallen Angels* indicates the importance of this symbol in the novel. Using clues from the text, consider what "angels" might symbolize in the novel.

Chapter 6

The Domino Theory

When TV camera crews interview members of the squad about their reasons for fighting, Lobel mentions "the domino theory, how if Vietnam fell to the Communists then the rest of Asia might fall" (p. 65). This comment echoed an expression, first coined by President Eisenhower in 1954, to describe the spread of communism.

Eisenhower believed that, if unchecked, communism from the Soviet Union and China would gather momentum. The communist takeover of one country in Southeast Asia would cause the rest of the Asian countries to fall under Communist control, toppling one by one like a row of dominoes—first Vietnam, then Laos and Cambodia, followed by Thailand and Burma. Three presidents after Eisenhower—Kennedy, Johnson, and Nixon—also cited the domino theory to justify U.S. military involvement in Vietnam.

Chapter 9

LITERARY CONCEPT

Euphemism

A euphemism is an expression that is used to disguise the unpleasant meaning associated with a more direct word. For example, "passed away" is a euphemism for "died."

However, some euphemisms can be deceptive. During the Vietnam War, the purpose of "pacification missions" was to promote goodwill and trust and "to win the hearts and minds of the people." In his famous essay "Politics and the English Language," written in 1946, George Orwell explores the sinister use of euphemisms such as pacification:

> **"In our time, political speech and writing are largely the defense of the indefensible. . . . Thus political language has to consist largely of euphemism, question-begging, and sheer cloudy vagueness. Defenseless villages are bombarded from the air, the inhabitants driven out into the countryside, the cattle machine-gunned, the huts set on fire with incendiary bullets: this is called *pacification.*"**

In *Fallen Angels*, Peewee also sees through the veiled meaning of this euphemism when he says, "Pacify them [the villagers] to death!" (p. 101).

Chapters 6, 11

The Living-Room War

The Vietnam War was also television's war. For the first time in American history, television cameras recorded the battles and then shipped the videotapes to the United States, where they were immediately broadcast on the evening news. In the comfort of their living rooms, television audiences learned about the day-to-day routine—and horror—of fighting a war.

The shocking images flashing across their screens had a powerful effect on viewers. Some were outraged and began criticizing U.S. military involvement. Others attacked the media, claiming that television trivialized the war by turning it into a never-ending prime-time drama. Questions about the effects of television coverage of the war still remain.

Chapter 12

The Protest Movement: "Hell, No, We Won't Go"

The members of Perry's squad hotly debate the issue of "guys burning their draft cards," reorted in Walowick's newspaper. This news story reflects the growing opposition to the Vietnam War back in the United States. The protest movement took various forms. Young Americans staged antiwar demonstrations, picketing induction centers and carrying signs that read "Burn Draft Cards—Not People," "Bring the Troops Home," and "Stop the Bombing." Sit-ins and strikes erupted on college campuses, especially after student draft deferments were abolished in early 1966 for college students ranking in the lower part of their class. Also, once deferred students had graduated from college, they could be drafted. By 1968, about 10,000 Americans had fled to Canada in order to avoid serving in a war they considered immoral.

Chapter 13

The Civil Rights Movement

In the 1960s, African Americans in the United States continued their long-time struggle for equality. During this time, the civil rights leader Dr. Martin Luther King, Jr., argued that equal opportunity could be achieved through nonviolent actions. His efforts helped prompt changes in laws. President Johnson showed his support of the civil rights movement when he signed the following two bills:

- The Civil Rights Act of 1964 prohibited forms of segregation, as well as job discrimination based on race, sex, and religion.

- The Voting Rights Act of 1965 authorized federal officials to ensure that voting procedures did not discriminate against African Americans.

Despite these political gains, many African Americans still felt that the wheels of justice were turning too slowly. In *Fallen Angels*, Perry notes the impact of the growing racial tensions in the United States on the soldiers fighting in Vietnam: "Back home the World seemed to be splitting up between people who wanted to make love and people who wanted to tear the cities down. A lot of it was blacks against whites, and we didn't talk about that too much, but we felt it. Over the summer a kid in Harlem had been killed by a white police sergeant and there had been some riots" (p. 128).

Dr. Martin Luther King, Jr., also drew a parallel between the violence of the war in Vietnam and the violence of the race riots erupting in American cities. In his last published essay, "A Testament of Hope" (1968), he wrote, ". . . bombs in Vietnam also explode at home; they destroy the hopes and possibilities for a decent America."

Chapter 13

The Tet Offensive

Perry remarks, "When the Tet started, we were put on alert" (p. 130). He is referring here to the Tet Offensive, the campaign masterminded by General Vo Nguyen Giap. This military strategy was reminiscent of one of the general's favorite tales—the legend of the Trojan horse. During the Trojan War, the Greeks devised a scheme to storm the city of Troy. They tricked the Trojans into dragging a gigantic, hollow wooden horse, filled with Greek warriors, into the city. Later that night, while the Trojans lay asleep, the Greek soldiers sprang their surprise attack and torched the city.

In a similar way, Giap's strategy was to conceal weapons and ammunition inside wooden coffins. An unusually large number of funeral processions were occurring before the Tet holiday. Vietcong, posing as mourners, paraded alongside the coffins. On January 30, 1968, the surprise attack was launched, stunning the Americans. The enemy attacked about 100 towns and cities, including Saigon and Hue, and 12 U.S. air bases. After less than a month of fighting, South Vietnamese and American troops succeeded in gaining control. In purely military terms, the Tet Offensive was not a success, but its effect on U.S. perception of the war marked a turning point in the conflict.

VOCABULARY

Alphabet Soup

KIA	Killed in action
ARVN	Army of the Republic of Vietnam
LZ	Landing Zone
NVA	North Vietnamese Army
PX	Post Exchange (the military store)
RPG	Rocket-propelled grenade

Chapter 14

The Five O'Clock Follies

What was the measure of winning the war in Vietnam? It was often a matter of simple arithmetic. As killing the enemy was the main objective, "body counts"—the total number of the enemy killed—became the gauge of success. The daily tally of dead enemies was one of the more gruesome aspects of the Vietnam War. Each day General Westmoreland, the U.S. military commander in South Vietnam, received body count reports from his generals. In turn, the generals had collected the body count figures from lower-ranking officers. To boost their reputations, officers at every level in the chain of command might inflate the numbers they reported to their superior officers. In *Fallen Angels*, Captain Stewart exaggerates the number of dead enemies, based on Perry's rough estimate.

News reporters in Saigon realized that such juggling of the body count figures was widespread. To them the official body count numbers, announced each day at Westmoreland's headquarters, were something of a joke. For this reason, reporters dubbed these daily briefings "the five o'clock follies."

Chapters 17–23

SECTION 4

Chapter 17

Double Bind

On the battlefields of Vietnam, African-American soldiers sometimes struggled with two enemies. One was the Vietcong; the other was racial prejudice. In *Fallen Angels*, Johnson's confrontation with Sergeant Dongan illustrates this struggle. Peewee tells Perry that Johnson asked Sergeant Dongan "how come he put a brother on point and another brother in the damn rear . . ." (p. 187). Johnson suspects that Dongan's decision to place both him and Peewee in such high-risk positions was an act of prejudice.

During the Vietnam War African-American soldiers, compared to white soldiers, were, in fact, more often assigned combat roles that jeopardized their lives. The following Defense Department statistics from 1967 support Dr. Martin Luther King, Jr.'s statement that African-American soldiers were fighting and dying "in extraordinarily high proportions relative to the rest of the population":

- 12.1% of total U.S. personnel in Vietnam were African American.

- 22.8% of total U.S. personnel with combat assignments were white.

- 28.6% of total U.S. personnel with combat assignments were African American.

- From 1965–1967 African Americans made up 23 percent of the total war casualties.

Chapter 22

A Deadly Game Of Hide-and-Seek

While on a night patrol, Perry asks himself, "Were the Congs creeping up on us? Could they see in the dark? Could they wrap the shadows around themselves and make themselves invisible?" (p. 242). These questions about the Vietcong's apparently superhuman powers typify the frustration and terror U.S. forces faced during jungle warfare. The Vietcong were masters in the art of concealment. They remained unseen amidst the dense foliage. Seeming to appear out of nowhere, they ambushed American troops and then retreated from sight. The Vietcong also hid in camouflaged foxholes called "spider holes," which were often linked to underground tunnels, some with an intricate network of passageways.

Chapter 23

Coming Home: Fast Forward

The Vietnam War was essentially a loner's war. Soldiers, like the fictional Richie Perry, arrived in Vietnam one by one and, after completing their tour of duty, were jetted home one by one. What might Perry experience following his plane ride aboard the "Freedom Bird" back to "the World"? For Vietnam veterans the abrupt shift from soldier to civilian— "from firefight to front porch in 36 hours," according to author Myra MacPherson—was extremely unsettling. They had no time to unwind or to reflect on their experiences. Unlike veterans of previous wars, Vietnam veterans did not receive a hero's homecoming—no cheering crowds or victory parades. Instead, many were greeted with indifference or hostility. This lack of recognition prolonged the healing process that all returning soldiers undergo.

The War Ends

In 1973, during President Nixon's administration, the United States and North Vietnam signed a cease-fire agreement. However, despite the withdrawal of American troops, fighting continued in Vietnam. A major North Vietnamese offensive swept through South Vietnam in March 1975. The South Vietnamese army collapsed, and the Communists entered Saigon the following month. U.S. involvement in Vietnam finally ended with the helicopter evacuation of the last remaining Americans.

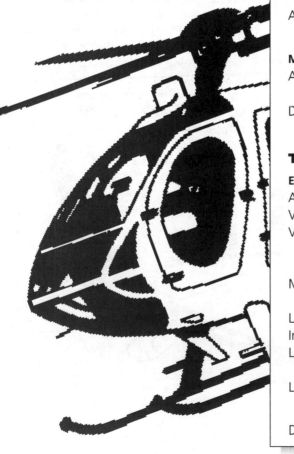

The Final Analysis

The numbers below provide a statistical overview of the United States' longest war.

The Commitment

MILITARY PERSONNEL

Americans who served:	3,330,000
Americans killed:	58,271
killed in battle:	47,655
Americans wounded:	303,713
Americans taken prisoner:	839
Returned:	691
Escaped:	34
Died in captivity:	114
Americans still classified as missing (1965–1975):	2,477
Americans awarded the Medal of Honor:	238

MONEY

American aid to South Vietnam (1955-1975):	$24 billion
Direct American expenditures for the war:	$165 billion

The Aftermath

EVACUATION

Americans evacuated:	1,373
Vietnamese evacuated:	5,595
Value of U.S. military equipment seized by Communists:	$5 billion
Military and civilian dead (all forces):	1,313,000
Land defoliated:	5.2 million acres
Indochinese refugees:	9,000,000
Living U.S. veterans with Vietnam service:	2,700,000
Living U.S. veterans receiving government compensation:	500,000
Disabled U.S. veterans:	519,000

Source: The New York Times, April 30, 1985. Copyright © 1985 by The New York Times *Company. Reprinted by permission of the New York Times.*

The Things They Carried

BY TIM O'BRIEN

Background

Tim O'Brien served in Vietnam after graduating from college in 1968. He reflects: ". . . when the draft notice arrived after graduation, the old demons went to work almost instantly. I thought about Canada. I thought about jail. But in the end I could not bear the prospect of rejection: by my family, my country, my friends, my hometown. I would risk conscience and rectitude before risking the loss of love." After being wounded in combat, O'Brien received the Purple Heart and was promoted to sergeant.

In *The Things They Carried*, a series of interconnecting short stories about Vietnam, O'Brien sometimes blurs the line between fiction and nonfiction by featuring a character whose name is also Tim O'Brien.

War Is More than Hell

In the essay "How to Tell a True War Story," O'Brien identifies the features that he believes characterize an honest depiction of war. For example, a true war story never preaches a moral. Moreover, a true war story reveals the contradictions of war: "War is hell, but that's not half of it, because war is also mystery and terror and adventure and courage and discovery and holiness and pity and despair and longing and love. War is nasty; war is fun. War is thrilling; war is drudgery. War makes you a man; war makes you dead."

Return to Vietnam

In 1994 O'Brien returned to Vietnam and recorded his impressions in "The Vietnam in Me," published in the *New York Times Magazine*. In confronting his past, he comes to this realization: "Vietnam was more than terror. For me, at least, Vietnam was partly love. With each step, each light-year of a second, a foot soldier is always almost dead, or so it feels, and in such circumstances, you can't *help* but love. You love your mom and dad, the Vikings, hamburgers on the grill, your pulse, your future—everything that might be lost or never come to be. Intimacy with death carries with it a corresponding new intimacy with life. Jokes are funnier, green is greener."

LITERARY CONCEPT

Style

Style is the particular way in which a piece of literature is written. In "The Things They Carried," notice the musical effect of repeating the phrase "they carried" in the opening sentences of many of the paragraphs.

In the Forest at Night

BY DUC THANH, TRANSLATED BY THANH T. NGUYEN AND BRUCE WEIGL

Background

"In the Forest at Night" was one of the many poems discovered among enemy documents captured by the U.S. military. According to Than T. Nguyen, one of the translators of "In the Forest at Night," "all Vietnamese wrote poetry, especially when they were separated from their loved ones."

Family Ties

Most Vietnamese are members of an extended family, a closely knit unit consisting of three or four generations living together in the same household. The oldest male is deemed the head of the family, a position of status and respect. Younger members are taught to obey older members, and children assume responsibility for the care of aged parents. Many Vietnamese also believe they have ties to their dead ancestors, whose spirits live on in the bodies of their children and grandchildren.

On Translation

The translators of "In the Forest at Night" are Bruce Weigl, a poet and a Vietnam veteran, and Thanh T. Nguyen, a Vietnamese-American college instructor. Their task involved far more than simply translating the poem word for word. Such literal translations often do not make sense because some words in Vietnamese do not have exact English equivalents. To retain the spirit of the original, which is printed on pages 299–300, the translators strove to recast the poem in English using language that captured the meaning and emotions conveyed in the Vietnamese.

A House Divided

Quoting from the Bible, Abraham Lincoln remarked in 1858, "A house divided against itself cannot stand." He was referring to the regional and political differences between the North and South, which, in 1860, evolved into the Civil War. The war not only split the nation but also split families. Sometimes brothers fought brothers and fathers fought sons.

In some ways, the situation in Vietnam mirrored the conditions of the American Civil War. Vietnam was also a "house divided," consisting of opposing groups from the North and South who fought one another in a bloody conflict. Duc Thanh, the soldier-poet who wrote "In the Forest at Night," fought on the side of North Vietnam.

What Were They Like?

BY DENISE LEVERTOV

Background

Denise Levertov was born in England in 1923. She served as an army nurse during World War II. Shortly after publishing her first book of poetry, *The Double Image,* in 1946, she moved to the United States and later became an American citizen. As an antiwar activist, Levertov remarked in 1965, "The poem has a social effect of some kind whether or not the poet wills it to have. It has a kinetic force, it sets in motion . . . elements in the reader that would otherwise be stagnant."

Political Poetry

As witnesses to the political events of their day, many poets have expressed their views about issues that concern them. Poet Kenneth Koch believes that writing political poetry poses special challenges: "To be a political poet, a poet with a cause, is in one way wonderful and inspiring. You have a theme you believe in, strong feelings, a reason to write. . . . The problem in writing poetry about a cause is how to remain yourself, how to be personal enough so that your own thoughts and feelings can get into the poem—feelings which may be contradictory and which may include questions and doubts . . ."

"Had They an Epic Poem?"

The speaker's response to this question is "It is not remembered" (line 19). In fact, an 18th-century Vietnamese scholar, Nguyen Du, composed *Kim Van Kieu,* a moving epic considered the national poem of the Vietnamese people.

An epic is a long narrative poem about the adventures of a hero or heroine whose actions reflect the values and concerns of a nation or race. Nguyen Du's epic tells of the heroine Kieu's quest to find her first love. To many Vietnamese people, her ultimate success represents the struggles and ordeals of their own country.

What Happened to the "Rice and Bamboo"?

In an effort to destroy the jungles that provided cover for the Vietcong, the U.S. military sprayed huge quantities of toxic chemicals. These defoliants, which caused leaves to drop off of plants, destroyed more than just the jungle: they devastated about 30 percent of the landscape. Until 1967, South Vietnam had been a major exporter of rice. By 1968, it was importing rice in an effort to prevent mass starvation.

look at this)

BY E. E. CUMMINGS

Background

E. E. Cummings (Edward Estlin Cummings) was an innovative modern poet whose work influenced many later writers. As a young man, he volunteered for duty in France during World War I and served in the Ambulance Corps. His prose book *The Enormous Room* is considered to be an outstanding literary account of World War I. Following the war, he remained in Paris to study art. Cummings remarked, "So far as I am concerned, poetry and every other art was and is and forever will be strictly and distinctly a question of individuality."

The Poetic Laboratory

Experimental poets like E. E. Cummings investigate new ways of using words and, in the process, "break the rules" of traditional forms of poetry. In his poems, Cummings often ignores rules of standard punctuation and capitalization, and uses parentheses in an unusual way. Sometimes he creates new words or spellings, runs words together, and stretches syllables over several lines. As you read Cummings's poetry, think about how his unconventional style affects meaning.

Poets from the Trenches: A Who's Who

E. E. Cummings was among the many poets whose writings often expressed views of World War I. Other notable soldier-poets, whose insights about the conditions of war still ring true today, include:

- Siegfried Sassoon (1886–1967)
- Wilfred Owen (1893–1918)
- Rupert Brooke (1887–1915)
- Isaac Rosenberg (1890–1918)

Firsts of the First World War

The term *75,* in line 2 of the poem, refers to a 75-millimeter gun. This weapon and other technology of warfare added a new dimension to the horrors of combat in World War I. Here is a list of innovations that distinguished World War I from previous wars:

- extensive use of machine guns
- poison gas and gas masks
- barbed wire
- steel helmets
- tanks
- fighter planes

The Spoils of War

BY LYNNE SHARON SCHWARTZ

Background

This article was first published in October, 1980—about five years after the Vietnam War had ended and about one month before Ronald Reagan became president. Just months earlier, Reagan had said about the Vietnam War, "It is time we recognized that ours, in truth, was a noble cause."

From Battlefield to Classroom

The GI Bill is the popular name of a program that began in 1944. It provides partial funding and benefits for United States veterans, including education and basic living expenses. Many Vietnam veterans like the one profiled in "The Spoils of War" took advantage of the GI Bill. Roughly two-thirds of soldiers returning from Vietnam became college students.

Post-Traumatic Stress Disorder

Veterans' psychological problems are the invisible wounds inflicted by wars. However, the terminology for these problems has changed over time: "shell shock" (World War I), "battle fatigue" (World War II and the Korean War), and "post-traumatic stress disorder" (Vietnam War). Sufferers of this syndrome might experience nightmares and flashbacks, feel panic-stricken, or withdraw emotionally from the people around them.

Image Makeover

Author Michael Lee Lanning, a Vietnam veteran, often visits high school classrooms. Here are some questions that students typically ask him:

• Do you have flashbacks?

• Can you sleep at night or do bad dreams keep you awake?

• Are all of you Vietnam veterans crazy?

• Have you ever thought of killing yourself?

These questions reflect common images of Vietnam veterans as disturbed men, haunted by memories. But how accurate are these images? In March 1985, the *Washington Post* and ABC News conducted a survey comparing Vietnam veterans to nonveterans. The findings showed that veterans were more likely to be college-educated homeowners. In addition, over 70 percent of the veterans polled said that they did not experience dreams of being back in Vietnam.

from Ghosts in the Wall

BY KRIS HARDIN

Background

Jan Scruggs, who set plans for the memorial in motion, was sent to Vietnam in 1969. Like Richie Perry, he couldn't afford to go to college and believed he was doing his patriotic duty by enlisting. After being wounded in action, Scruggs returned. "Back at home," he states, "I found my fellow veterans were being scorned for fighting in an unpopular war. Few people wanted to be reminded about the brave soldiers who died because their country asked them to serve."

Inscription on the Memorial

IN HONOR OF THE MEN AND WOMEN OF THE ARMED FORCES OF THE UNITED STATES WHO SERVED IN THE VIETNAM WAR. THE NAMES OF THOSE WHO GAVE THEIR LIVES AND OF THOSE WHO REMAIN MISSING ARE INSCRIBED IN THE ORDER THEY WERE TAKEN FROM THE US.

OUR NATION HONORS THE COURAGE, SACRIFICE AND DEVOTION TO DUTY AND COUNTRY OF ITS VIETNAM VETERANS. THIS MEMORIAL WAS BUILT WITH PRIVATE CONTRIBUTIONS FROM THE AMERICAN PEOPLE.
NOVEMBER 11, 1982

Tokens of Grief

The National Park Service's Museum Archeological Regional Storage Facility (MARS) in Lanham, Maryland, houses the thousands of mementos that have been left at the Memorial. David Guynes, the curator of MARS, calls these items "the material of social history. . . . So many stories are in them, so much feeling, emotion, heartache." Here is just a sampling of those items.

• tiny American flags

• grenade pins

• stuffed animals and toy

• notes and greeting cards

• record albums

• high school photographs

• cheerleaders' pom-poms

• soldiers' gear

An Added Remembrance

Kris Hardin's essay states that later on a "flag and a statue would be placed to one side" of the memorial. On Veterans Day, 1984, a bronze statue of three soldiers— an African American, a white, and a Hispanic—was dedicated. The sculptor of the statue, Frederick Hart, remarked, "The portrayal of the figures is consistent with history. . . . The contrast between the innocence of their youth and the weapons of war underscores the poignancy of their sacrifice."

Glossary

Section 1: Chapters 1–5

armorer (är'mər-ər) *n.* an enlisted person who is responsible for maintaining and repairing the small arms of his military unit *p. 29*

black market (blăk mär'kĭt) *n.* the illegal buying or selling of goods *p. 18*

charred (chärd) *adj.* burnt or scorched *p. 34*

DDT *n.* a powerful insecticide, banned in 1972 out of concern for its effects on humans and animals *p. 18*

fatigues (fə-tēgz') *n.* work clothes worn by soldiers *p. 34*

hooch (hōoch) *n.* slang: for soldiers' simple dwelling *p. 15*

insignia (ĭn-sĭg'nē-ə) *n.* a badge of rank or membership *p. 22*

intelligence (ĭn-tĕl'ə-jəns) *n.* people who collect secret information about an enemy *p. 33*

jive (jīv) *v.* slang: to play or joke around *p. 31*

latrine (lə-trēn') *n.* a toilet to be used by a large number of people, as in an army camp *p. 26*

makeshift* (māk'shĭft') *adj.* crude *p. 49*

malaria (mə-lâr'ē-ə) *n.* an infectious disease transmitted by mosquitoes *p. 18*

orientation (ôr'ē-ĕn-tā'shən) *n.* an adaptation or adjustment to a new situation or to new surroundings *p. 16*

phosphorus (fŏs'fər-əs) *n.* a highly reactive element used in explosive devices *p. 42*

shard* (shärd) *n.* a small piece of a brittle material, such as metal or glass *p. 35*

shrapnel (shrăp'nəl) *n.* fragments scattered by an explosive device *p. 23*

surveillance (sər-vā'ləns) *n.* close observation, often of an enemy or someone under suspicion *p. 33*

theology* (thē-ŏl'ə-jē) *n.* the study of God and religious faith *p. 38*

truce* (trōos) *n.* a temporary stop to the fighting between two opposing sides *p. 15*

Section 2: Chapters 6–11

barrage (bə-räzh') *n.* artillery fire directed in front of friendly troops to provide them with cover from the enemy *p. 86*

cache* (kăsh) *n.* a place where something valuable is hidden *p. 111*

cordite (kôr'dīt') *n.* an explosive powder *p. 80*

correspondent* (kôr'ĭ-spŏn'dənt) *n.* a person hired by a newspaper, news agency, or magazine to write news articles *p. 70*

firefight (fīr'fīt') *n.* a battle involving the exchange of small artillery fire with the enemy *p. 60*

frag (frăg) *v.* military slang: to intentionally kill or wound someone *p. 97*

hamlet* (hăm'lĭt) *n.* a very small town or village *p. 93*

infiltrate* (ĭn'fĭl-trāt') *v.* to penetrate an area or group gradually or stealthily *p. 118*

intricate (ĭn'trĭ-kĭt) *adj.* elaborate or complexly arranged *p. 59*

PRONUNCIATION KEY

ă	at, gas	îr	dear, here	th	thing, with
ā	ape, day	ng	sing, anger	th	then, other
ä	father, barn	ŏ	odd, not	ŭ	up, nut
âr	fair, dare	ō	open, road, grow	ûr	fur, earn, bird, worm
ĕ	egg, ten	ô	awful, bought, horse	zh	treasure, garage
ē	evil, see, meal	oi	coin, boy	ə	awake, even, pencil, pilot, focus
hw	white, everywhere	ŏŏ	look, full		
ĭ	inch, fit	ōō	root, glue, through	ər	perform, letter
ī	idle, my, tried	ou	out, cow		

SOUNDS IN FOREIGN WORDS

kh	*German* ich, auch; *Scottish* loch	œ	*French* feu, cœur; *German* schön	ü	*French* utile, rue; *German* grün
n	*French* entre, bon, fin				

* The words followed by asterisks are useful words that you might add to your vocabulary.

Glossary (continued)

plasma (plăz′mə) *n.* the portion of the blood used in giving transfusions *p. 87*

protrusion (prō-trōō′zhən) *n.* a thing that juts out *p. 59*

reconnaissance (rĭ-kŏn′ə-səns) *n.* an exploratory search for information about enemy positions or installations *p. 116*

reverent (rĕv′ər-ənt) *adj.* showing awe and respect *p. 111*

shelling (shĕl′ĭng) *n.* a bombardment from a large gun or guns *p. 87*

tracer (trā′sər) *n.* a bullet that leaves a trace of smoke or fire to help in readjusting one's aim *p. 86*

Section 3: Chapters 12–16

bivouac (bĭv′ōō-ăk′) *v.* to camp in a temporary encampment, often without shelter *p. 161*

brief* (brēf) *v.* to advise or to summarize instructions *p. 146*

casualty* (kăzh′ōō-əl-tē) *n.* a soldier who has been killed or wounded *p. 125*

concussion (kən-kŭsh′ən) *n.* an injury to the brain resulting from a sharp blow to the head *p. 174*

coordinate (kō-ôr′dən-āt′) *n.* the exact location of a point in a designated space *p. 131*

deploy (dĭ-ploi′) *v.* to station military forces in a certain area *p. 132*

guerrilla (gə-rĭl′ə) *n.* a member of a small, irregular military unit that harrasses the enemy with tactics such as surprise attacks *p. 129*

harassment* (hə-răs′mənt) *n.* the procedure of inflicting damage on enemy forces by repeatedly attacking them *p. 146*

interdiction (ĭn′tər-dĭk′shən) *n.* the act of prohibiting, restraining, or hindering an action *p. 130*

mortar (môr′tər) *n.* a small, portable cannon used to fire shells over short ranges *p. 137*

numbers man (nŭm′bərz măn) *n.* someone who operates an illegal betting game *p. 123*

phantom (făn′təm) *adj.* illusory; appearing only in the mind *p. 149*

reinforce* (rē′ĭn-fôrs′) *v.* to strengthen *p. 168*

skirmish* (skûr′mĭsh) *n.* a brief military encounter; a fight *p. 170*

vigilance* (vĭj′ə-ləns) *n.* alertness to danger; watchfulness *p. 146*

Section 4: Chapters 17–23

adhesion (ăd-hē′zhən) *n.* the abnormal joining of body tissues that should be separate *p. 260*

Buddha (bōō′də) *n.* the name given to the Indian philosopher and teacher who founded

Buddhism, the religion followed by most of the Vietnamese people *p. 238*

contingent (kən-tĭn′jənt) *n.* a group of soldiers, forming part of a larger group *p. 206*

cosmolene (kŏz′mə-lēn′) *n.* a heavy-grade petroleum product used as a protective coating on firearms *p. 234*

forced march (fôrst märch) *n.* a march taken at a faster pace than usual *p. 210*

impassively* (ĭm-păs′ĭv-lē) calmly; in a way that shows no emotion or feeling *p. 215*

maximize (măk′sə-mīz) *v.* to increase *p. 194*

napalm (nā′päm) *n.* an incendiary substance used in bombs and flame throwers *p. 208*

nondenominational (nŏn′dĭ-nŏm′ə-nā′shə-nəl) *adj.* not affiliated with a particular religious body or organization *p. 234*

projectile (prə-jĕk′təl) *n.* an object shot through the air, as a bullet, shell, or piece of shrapnel *p. 255*

requisition* (rĕk′wĭ-zĭsh′ən) *v.* to make a written request *p. 193*

veer* (vîr) *v.* to shift or change direction *p. 253*

* The words followed by asterisks are useful words that you might add to your vocabulary.

Strategic Reading ①

Tracking Characters

Many of the main characters in *Fallen Angels* are introduced in this section. Fill in the chart below to help you identify them. In the second column, note important details about each character's background—for example, where he comes from or what his rank is. In the third column, note the character's personality traits.

CHARACTER	BACKGROUND	PERSONALITY TRAITS
Richie Perry		
Peewee Gates		
Lieutenant Carroll		
Jenkins		
Johnson		
Sergeant Simpson		
Monaco		
Lobel		
Walowick		

Drawing Conclusions

By interpreting specific incidents in a realistic novel, you can draw more general conclusions about the events depicted. The chart below summarizes key events that occur in this section. Complete the chart by drawing a conclusion based on the significance of each event.

CHAPTER	KEY EVENT	DRAW A CONCLUSION ABOUT:
6	A television news team interviews members of Perry's squad.	Reasons for fighting the Vietnam War: _____ _____ _____
7	Walowick, a white soldier, fights with Johnson, an African-American soldier.	Tensions and conflicts within the squad: _____ _____ _____
8	While on patrol, one U.S. platoon opens fire at another U.S. platoon.	The blunders of war: _____ _____ _____
9	Perry's platoon goes on a peace mission to a nearby village.	The soldiers' views toward the Vietnamese: _____ _____ _____
10	Lieutenant Carroll is killed during an ambush.	The realities of combat: _____ _____ _____
11	The platoon mourns the loss of Carroll.	Coping with death during wartime: _____ _____ _____

Analyzing Cause-and-Effect Relationships

Characters' actions can sometimes cause different consequences, or effects. Use this diagram to help you better understand how some major events in this section of the novel are related. Below each box, write one or more effects that stem from that cause.

Cause: ➜	Effect(s):
1. On Lieutenant Gearhart's first mission with the platoon, he accidentally shoots off a flare.	

Cause: ➜	Effect(s):
2. On Gearhart's mission, Perry first forgets to set up claymores (explosive devices), then turns them the wrong way.	

Cause: ➜	Effect(s):
3. Gearhart's platoon secures a village infiltrated with Vietcong.	

Cause: ➜	Effect(s):
4. To increase body counts, Captain Stewart has been volunteering the platoon for combat patrols.	

Analyzing Character

Richie Perry experiences a wide range of emotions as events unfold in this final section of the novel. Next to each feeling on the chart below, summarize events that cause Perry to feel this way. You may cite more than one event for each emotion.

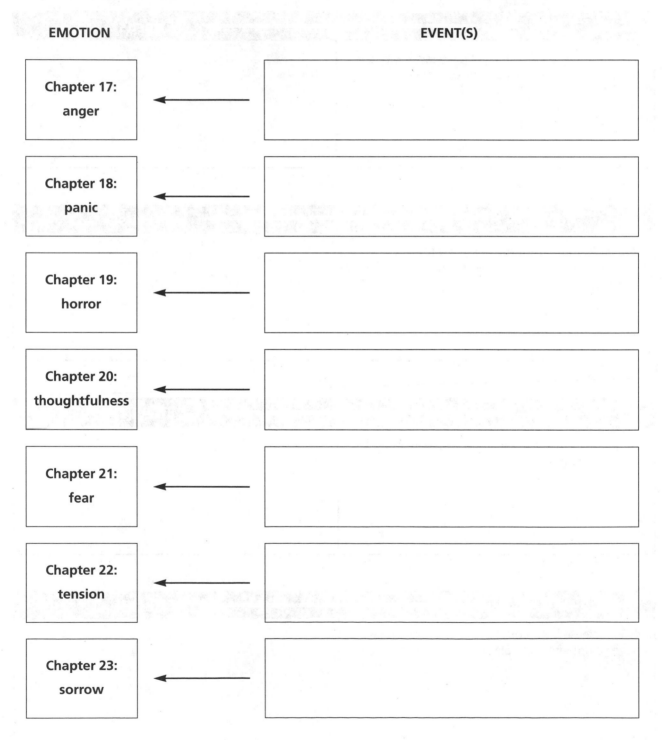

EMOTION	EVENT(S)
Chapter 17: anger	
Chapter 18: panic	
Chapter 19: horror	
Chapter 20: thoughtfulness	
Chapter 21: fear	
Chapter 22: tension	
Chapter 23: sorrow	

Literary Concept

THEME

The theme of a literary work is an insight about life or human experience that the writer presents to the reader. The following statements represent different aspects of the novel's theme of war and its impact. Rate your response to each statement before and after you read the novel by marking an X and an O on each continuum. Then explain why the novel did or did not change your point of view. Finally, compare your ideas with those of your classmates.

1. Young soldiers engaged in combat typically undergo a personal transformation—a passage from youth to maturity, from innocence to experience.

(x = Before reading, o = After reading)

STRONGLY AGREE   STRONGLY DISAGREE

Comments: _____

_____

2. Warfare often forces soldiers to reconsider their traditional notions of right and wrong.

(x = Before reading, o = After reading)

STRONGLY AGREE   STRONGLY DISAGREE

Comments: _____

_____

3. The conditions of war show the true nature of heroism.

(x = Before reading, o = After reading)

STRONGLY AGREE   STRONGLY DISAGREE

Comments: _____

_____

4. Friendships and bonds are often intensified among people who face constant danger and the threat of sudden death.

(x = Before reading, o = After reading)

STRONGLY AGREE   STRONGLY DISAGREE

Comments: _____

_____

5. War brings out extremes of behavior—not only courage, loyalty, and sacrifice but also brutality, prejudice, and arrogance.

(x = Before reading, o = After reading)

STRONGLY AGREE   STRONGLY DISAGREE

Comments: _____

_____

6. War is chaotic: Soldiers often find it difficult to make sense of or find meaning in combat.

(x = Before reading, o = After reading)

STRONGLY AGREE   STRONGLY DISAGREE

Comments: _____

_____

7. The experiences of war may leave long-lasting emotional scars on soldiers, civilians, and nations.

(x = Before reading, o = After reading)

STRONGLY AGREE   STRONGLY DISAGREE

Comments: _____

_____

Name _____

Characterization refers to the methods a writer uses to develop characters. Choose a character from _Fallen Angels_ that you want to profile. Then fill in the diagram below with details from the novel that show what that character is like. Think about how different traits fit together to create the whole character.

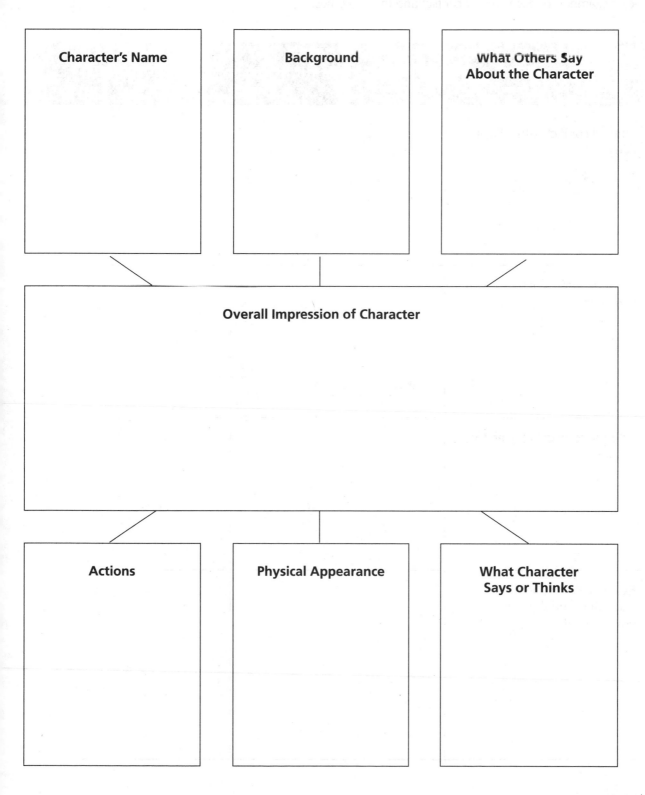

| Character's Name | Background | What Others Say About the Character |

Overall Impression of Character

| Actions | Physical Appearance | What Character Says or Thinks |

Literary Concept ③

CONFLICT

As a war novel, *Fallen Angels* is filled with conflicts, or struggles between opposing forces. An **external conflict** involves a character pitted against an outside force, such as nature, a physical obstacle, or another character. An **internal conflict** is a struggle that occurs within a character. Fill out the chart below with specific examples of each type of conflict and the outcomes.

TYPE OF CONFLICT	EXAMPLES FROM THE NOVEL	OUTCOME(S)
Internal conflict within Richie Perry		
External conflict between two characters		
External conflict between two groups		
External conflict between characters and the physical environment		

Vocabulary

A. Complete the crossword below, using the asterisked words from the Glossary for *Fallen Angels*.

1. A guard on sentry duty must show this quality.

2. If something is made to be this way, it won't last long.

3. This place is much smaller than a city.

4. This sliver may be metal or glass.

5. The enemy stealthily entering a camp does this.

6. Something is hidden here.

B. Next write the clues for this completed crossword.

1. _____
_____

2. _____
_____

3. _____
_____

4. _____
_____

5. _____
_____

6. _____
_____

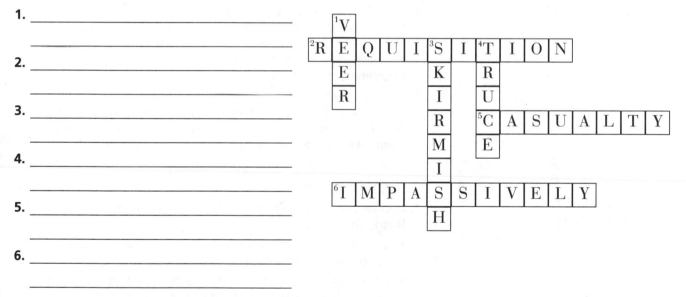

C. Create a third crossword, using the remaining asterisked words from the Glossary. Give your crossword to a partner to complete.

Beyond the Literature

Culminating Writing Assignments

EXPLORATORY WRITING

1. During the Vietnam War, American soldiers fought in a land that was unfamiliar and strange to them. Rewrite an incident from *Fallen Angels* as a **scene** from a science fiction story about aliens fighting a strange enemy in a strange land.

2. Write a **letter of commendation** that Perry might receive from the army upon his return home. The letter should assess his performance as a soldier and note courageous actions deserving of high praise.

3. Imagine you are a news reporter assigned to cover the Vietnam War. Using details from the novel, write a **feature article** profiling a day in the life of a U.S. soldier.

RESEARCH

1. Write a **research report** on a topic inspired by the novel or related to the Vietnam War. Examples include the domino theory, the Gulf of Tonkin incident, the Paris peace talks, the Tet Offensive, the anti-war movement, the postwar problems of Vietnam veterans, Vietnamese refugees, and so on.

2. Research the role African-American soldiers played in another war—for example, the Revolutionary War, the Civil War, World War I, World War II, the Korean War, or the Persian Gulf War. Write a **summary** highlighting their contributions in that war.

LITERARY ANALYSIS

1. Choose one of the following statements that are part of the novel's theme about war:

   • Warfare often forces soldiers to reconsider their traditional notions of right and wrong.

   • Friendships and bonds are often intensified among people who face constant danger and the threat of sudden death.

   • The conditions of war show the true nature of heroism.

   Then choose at least two characters from the novel and write a **critical essay** explaining how the statement is revealed through these characters' actions and behavior.

2. Write a **comparison** between *Fallen Angels* and one of the related readings in this book. Compare the two pieces by concentrating on a specific literary element such as theme, conflict, or characterization.

3. Choose one of the quotations from the "Critic's Corner" provided by your teacher. Write an **opinion essay** stating whether or not you agree with that critic, supporting your views with evidence from the novel.

* For writing instruction in specific modes, have students use the **Writing Coach.**

Multimodal Activities

The Numbers Game

Historians have gathered an enormous amount of numerical data pertaining to the Vietnam War and its aftermath. Encourage students to research the "numbers"—percentages, statistics, amounts of money, and so on—for a particular topic related to the war. Examples include U.S. war costs, opinion polls about the war, Vietnam War veterans, prisoners of war, and Vietnamese refugees. Then have interested students create **visual aids**—graphs, tables, and charts—that display the numerical data they have researched. Post the visual aids on a classroom bulletin board.

Soundtrack

Musicians and musical groups mentioned in *Fallen Angels* include Ramsey Lewis, Wilson Pickett, Jimi Hendrix, Mary Wells, the Shirelles, the Temptations, Diana Ross from the Supremes, and Smokey Robinson and the Miracles. Recordings by these artists and others from the 1960s may be available at public libraries. Have students work as a class or in small groups to create an **audiotape** of a musical soundtrack for *Fallen Angels* by recording and arranging different cuts from this music of the 60s.

Vietnam Revisited

Have students research Vietnam today and then create a **travel brochure** to attract tourists. Suggest that students include a map of historic sites in their brochure. If your students have access to the Internet, they could use this to conduct their research.

Hawks and Doves

Encourage students to role-play "Hawks"—those who supported the Vietnam War—and "Doves"—those who opposed it. Have each group create **posters** with slogans that support its cause. Suggest that students research actual pro-war or anti-war slogans, such as "America— Love It or Leave It," and "Give Peace a Chance." Then ask pairs of "hawks" and "doves" to hold informal discussions in which they give support for their positions.

Dateline: Those Turbulent 60s

To broaden students' understanding of the political, social, and cultural climate of the 1960s, have them work in small groups to create **time lines** highlighting important issues and events of this decade. Possible topics include the civil rights movement, the protest movement, the feminist revolution, trends in popular music, historic moments in space flight, sports highlights, best-selling books, and so on. Display their time lines on a bulletin board.

Eyewitness to History

Have the class invite a representative of a local Vietnam Veterans' organization to talk to the class about problems that soldiers faced both in Vietnam and in the United States upon their return. Students should prepare **interview questions** to pose to the guest speaker.

Vietspeak

Explain that the Vietnam War gave rise to hundreds of terms unique to that time and place. Have interested students research the military jargon, acronyms, and slang expressions used during the Vietnam War and create a class **glossary** of the terms. Encourage them to include examples from *Fallen Angels*.

Comedy Club

Have interested students write and present **comedy routines** inspired by humorous scenes in *Fallen Angels*, particularly those featuring Peewee Gates, who provides much of the humor in the novel. Advise students to approach the topic with sensitivity, but remind them that humor has often been employed to examine highly serious topics. Some students may choose to work individually and perform as stand-up comics. Others may opt to work in pairs or small groups and perform skits. For ideas, students could watch TV sitcoms that poke fun at war, such as *M*A*S*H* or *Hogan's Heroes*. If possible, you may wish to videotape students' performances.

Cross-Curricular Projects

A Memorial to the "Fallen Angels"

Overview:

In this project, groups of students design a war memorial paying tribute to the characters who lost their lives in *Fallen Angels*.

Cross-Curricular Connections: Art, History, Political Science

Suggested Procedure:

1. Tell students that they are going to design a memorial to honor the following characters who were killed in *Fallen Angels*: Jenkins, Lieutenant Carroll, Brew, Turner, Sergeant Dongan, and Judy Duncan. Have them discuss feelings or ideas that they think the memorial should communicate.

2. Allow students time to research examples of war memorials. Then have them brainstorm possible designs.

3. Divide students into small groups to plan their designs for the memorial. Suggest they begin by drawing a rough sketch. Then have groups think about the construction materials they might use, inscriptions they might include, and other relevant details. If possible, provide students with supplies they will need, such as paint, clay, cloth, posters, and so on.

4. Have each group work to build scale models or replicas of their war memorial.

5. Invite the groups to present their designs to the class and discuss why they think they are fitting memorials to the characters in *Fallen Angels*.

Teaching Tip

You may wish to broaden this assignment by suggesting that each group also submit a written proposal describing the design and its purpose.

The Theater of War

Overview:

In this project, students will find letters, excerpts from memoirs, and poems written by Vietnam veterans. They will then perform dramatic readings of this literature for the class.

Cross-Curricular Connections: Drama, History

Suggested Procedure:

1. Ask students to form groups according to the type of writing they would like to dramatize—letters, excerpts from memoirs, or poems. Then have each group find books containing these genres. Allow time for students to choose examples that they find particularly insightful or moving.

2. Have the groups decide on the format, such as solo readings or choral readings, for presenting the works they have selected to dramatize.

3. Suggest that groups consider using costumes, props, set designs, and/or music during their performances.

4. After sufficient rehearsal time, have the groups perform their dramatic readings for the class. If students wish to videotape their readings, they can present the tapes instead of performing live.

Teaching Tip

Suggest that students might include oral readings of speeches by political leaders of the time, such as Lyndon Johnson, Richard Nixon, Robert Kennedy, Eugene McCarthy, and Dr. Martin Luther King, Jr.

Celebrate the Tet Holiday

Overview:

People in Southeast Asian countries, as well as Vietnamese Americans in the United States, observe the Tet holiday, celebrating the lunar new year. In this project, students research this holiday, and then plan and devise creative ways for celebrating Tet.

Cross-Curricular Connections: Art, Music, History, Cultural Anthropology

Suggested Procedure:

1. Explain to students that Tet, the lunar new year, is a special holiday in Southeast Asia. Tell them that the observance of Tet resembles a combination of some of our customary ways of celebrating the Fourth of July, Thanksgiving, and Christmas. Setting off fireworks, eating festive foods, exchanging gifts, and visiting with family and friends are all part of the Tet Celebration. Students could reread Chapter 12 of *Fallen Angels*, in which Richie Perry refers to Tet and the truce that was supposed to occur because of the holiday.

2. Have students research how Tet is celebrated. They could consult books or use the Internet, if possible. If you have students in your class who are Vietnamese Americans, invite them to share their experiences in commemorating this holiday.

3. Help students brainstorm a list of ideas for celebrating Tet. You may wish to suggest possibilities—for example, making colorful paper lanterns and other ornaments, setting up decorative booths, creating sound effects of exploding firecrackers, playing Vietnamese music, and eating special foods.

4. Divide students into small committees. Each committee should be responsible for one aspect of the celebration. Suggest that students research topics related to their committee's role in the celebration.

5. Allow students time to create artwork, prepare food, make audio-tapes, and so on. Then have each committee contribute the class celebration of Tet.

> ## Teaching Tip
>
> You could assign a team of students whose responsibility is to coordinate the activities of all the small committees.

Suggestions for Assessment

Negotiated Rubrics

Negotiating rubrics for assessment with students allows them to know before they start an assignment what is required and how it will be judged, and gives them additional ownership of the final product. A popular method of negotiating rubrics is for the teacher and students individually to list the qualities that the final product should contain, then compare the teacher-generated list with the student-generated list and together decide on a compromise.

Portfolio Building

Remind students that they have many choices of types of assignments to select for their portfolios. Among these are the following:

- Culminating Writing Assignments (page 50)
- Writing Prompts, found in the Discussion Starters
- Multimodal Activities (pages 51–52)
- Cross-Curricular Projects (pages 53–55)

Suggest that students use some of the following questions as criteria in selecting which pieces to include in their portfolios.

- Which shows my clearest thinking about the literature?
- Which is or could become most complete?
- Which shows a type of work not presently included in my portfolio?
- Which am I proudest of?

Remind students to reflect on the pieces they choose and to attach a note explaining why they included each and how they would evaluate it.

For suggestions on how to assess portfolios, see **Teacher's Guide to Assessment and Portfolio Use.**

Writing Assessment

The following can be made into formal assignments for evaluation:

- Culminating Writing Assignments page 50
- a written analysis of the Critic's Corner literary criticism
- fully developed Writing Prompts from the Discussion Starters

For rubrics to help you evaluate specific kinds of writing, see **The Guide to Writing Assessment** *in the* **Formal Assessment** *booklet of* **The Language of Literature.**

Test

The test on pages 57–58 consists of essay and short-answer questions. The answer key follows.

Alternative Assessment

For the kinds of authentic assessments found on many statewide and districtwide tests, see the **Alternative Assessment** booklet of **The Language of Literature.**

Essay

Choose two of the following essay questions to answer on your own paper. (25 points each)

1. In Chapter 18 of *Fallen Angels*, Richard Perry reflects on his war experiences: "Some parts you could laugh at . . . Other parts . . . you tried to shut out of your mind" (p. 198). Analyze how these two contrasting reactions—laughter and denial—help Perry and other characters endure the grim reality of war. Give examples from the novel to support your analysis.

2. In a book review published in the *New York Times,* critic Mel Watkins writes,

   Equally important to his [Richie Perry's] growth are the many people he encounters. . . . Mr. Myers has also peopled his novel with some refreshing, original characters. . . . Mr. Myers . . . [allows] his main characters to emerge as interesting, complex people, rather than just stereotyped soldiers. . . .

   Do you agree with this interpretation of the way characters are depicted in *Fallen Angels*? Support your opinion with examples from the novel.

3. In *Fallen Angels* Richie Perry matures rapidly, moving from innocence to experience during his tour of duty. Fill out the diagram below to help you explore how his character changes. In the box labeled "Innocence," write a sentence describing Perry's perspective before he has experienced combat. In the box labeled "Experience," write a sentence describing Perry's perspective after combat. Then list three combat events that you think are most responsible for Perry's change in perspective. Using the information in your diagram, write an essay analyzing the transformation of Perry's character.

RICHIE PERRY		
INNOCENCE	**COMBAT EVENTS**	**EXPERIENCE**
	1. 2. 3.	

4. How does the title *Fallen Angels* relate to what happens in the novel? What is symbolic about the title?

5. Choose one of the following pairs to compare and contrast:

   a. Lieutenant Carroll and Lieutenant Jimmy Cross in the short story "The Things They Carried"

   b. Richie Perry and George Olsen, author of the letter from *Dear America: Letters Home from Vietnam*

   c. the Vietnamese in *Fallen Angels* and the Vietnamese in the poem "What Were They Like?"

Short Answer

1. What aspects of the physical environment of Vietnam do the soldiers find especially difficult to cope with?

2. What do you think Richie Perry's letter to Lieutenant Carroll's wife reveals about his personality?

3. What are Lobel's personal reasons for enlisting in the army?

4. Write a brief definition of the word *friendship* from Perry's point of view.

5. What effects do Peewee's jokes have on the members of the squad?

6. What do you think is the most horrifying war scene depicted in the novel?

7. Think of a single adjective that, in your opinion, best describes Johnson's personality. Give a reason for your choice.

8. Give two examples of Dongan's behavior or character traits that negatively affect the morale and unity of his squad.

9. Why is Perry not totally honest with Kenny in his letters to him about his war experiences?

10. Name one positive and one negative effect on Perry's personality resulting from his service in the Vietnam War.

Essay

Answers to essay questions will vary, but opinions should be stated clearly and supported by details from the text. Suggestions for points to look for are given below.

1. Laughter eases the tension of the day-to-day stress of fighting the war and diverts the soldiers' attention from the grim situations they face. By denying, or shutting out their horrifying experiences, the soldiers can keep more focused on surviving and carrying out their duties in each new combat situation.

2. Students who agree with this judgment of the novel might point out that Myers depicts many sides of his characters. For example, he shows Perry in various roles—son, brother, friend, and soldier. Moreover, Peewee's jokes about the war reveal a deeper side of his character: He understands the absurdity inherent in war and the military way of life.

   Students who disagree with this judgment might say that some of Myers's characters lack dimension. For examples, some may think that Peewee has been typecast as the "class clown," that Sergeant Simpson is a stereotype of the tough, no-nonsense officer, and that some of Lieutenant Carroll's dialogue and behavior seem too good to be true.

3. Before combat, Richie Perry naively sees himself as a "good guy" whom the Vietnamese in the hamlets will like. However, after combat, he is no longer certain about the morality of what he is doing: "Maybe the time had passed when anybody could be a good guy" (p. 126). He is increasingly weary of the carnage and waste of human life around him. Some events that precipitate this changed perspective include Lieutenant Carroll's death, the killing of the Vietcong whose gun misfires, and the burning of the dead Americans' bodies.

4. Many students will point out that the title relates to Lieutenant Carroll's prayer about the "angel warriors who fall"—soldiers who are killed in combat. Richie Perry echoes this phrase two other times in the novel after soldiers, including Lieutenant Carroll, have died. The title *Fallen Angels* might also symbolize loss of life in the war, as well as the lost innocence of those who survive.

5. **a.** Lieutenant Carroll is portrayed as a generous and sensitive man, a trusted leader, and a comrade in battle. He has risked his life for his troops and died a hero. Throughout most of "The Things They Carried," Lieutenant Jimmy Cross appears to be wrapped up in himself and does not seem to instill discipline in his men. However, at the end of the story, he aspires to become a leader similar to Lieutenant Carroll.

   b. Both Richie Perry and George Olsen struggle with their consciences and feel guilty about killing the enemy. They also both need to communicate in writing their feelings and experiences about the war. Richie Perry, however, seems more sympathetic to people who oppose the war.

   c. The Vietnamese in *Fallen Angels* are rarely portrayed as individuals and their viewpoint is not presented. The Vietnamese in "What Were They Like?" are portrayed as human beings with a cultural identity and as the victims of unspeakable tragedies.

Short Answer

Answers will vary but should reflect the following ideas.

1. Aspects of the physical environment that are difficult to cope with include the insects, the dense foliage of the jungles, and the oppressive heat and humidity.

2. Perry's letter to Lieutenant Carroll's wife reveals his sympathetic and thoughtful nature. His careful choice of words and details to console Carroll's wife shows that he can express himself effectively in writing.

3. Lobel seems to have enlisted as a way of seeking approval from his father or of spiting him. Lobel apparently wants his father to recognize that fighting in the war is proof of his masculinity.

4. From Perry's point of view, friendship consists of loyalty, trust, mutual respect, and caring.

5. Though Peewee's jokes aren't always appreciated, they generally provide comic relief, while occasionally offering the squad members a glimpse of the absurdity of war.

6. Among the most horrifying scenes in the novel are the explosion of a mine-rigged child, the stripping and burning of slain soldiers' bodies to prevent their mutilation by the enemy, and the incident in which Perry shoots off the face of a Vietcong.

7. *Proud, dignified,* and *serious* are among some of the adjectives that aptly describe Johnson's personality. He prizes self-respect and is conscientious in carrying out his duties as a soldier.

8. Dongan's unfriendliness and prejudiced attitudes create tensions within the squad. These traits are illustrated when Dongan places both Peewee and Johnson in high-risk positions.

9. Perry wants to protect Kenny from learning about the harsh realities of combat and does not want him to romanticize the heroism of soldiers.

10. The experiences of combat have made Perry more mature, but they have placed on him the burden of guilt and knowledge of the horrors of war. The psychological wounds will take time to heal.

Additional Resources

Other Works by Walter Dean Myers

Hoops. 1983.
Urban teenager Lonnie Jackson just wants to play basketball. When an older friend becomes involved with gamblers, it is Lonnie who profits—not financially but from his friend's example.

The Outside Shot. 1987.
In this sequel to *Hoops,* Lonnie plays basketball at a Midwestern college and finds that his street smarts have not prepared him for tough classes and sports corruption.

Scorpions. 1987.
Twelve-year-old Tito struggles to cope with life when the Scorpions, a street gang, move in.

The Legend of Tarik. New York: Scholastic, 1987.
Based on a true story, this novel, set in Africa, presents the life of a Moorish general who led the Moors' conquest of Spain in 711. Cited as a 1982 Notable Children's Trade Book in Social Studies.

Now Is Your Time! The African-American Struggle for Freedom. 1991.
This nonfiction work explores the African-American experience from the time of slavery through the civil rights movement into the present.

The Glory Field. 1993.
This novel tells the saga of the Lewis family, from the 1700s to the present day. Their experiences represent milestones in African-American history.

FICTION

Caputo, Philip. *A Rumor of War.* New York: Ballantine, 1977. A story of men at war as told by a young midwesterner who comes of age in the jungles of Vietnam. **(challenge)**

Crane, Stephen. *The Red Badge of Courage*: *An Episode of the American Civil War.* Ed. Henry Binder. New York: Avon, 1979. A powerful account of a young Civil War soldier's initiation into the grim reality of combat. **(average)**

Hemingway, Ernest. *The Nick Adams Stories.* New York: Bantam, 1973. A collection of short stories chronicling the life of the fictional character Nick Adams, including his experiences as a World War I soldier and as a disillusioned veteran. **(average)**

O'Brien, Tim. *The Things They Carried.* Boston: Houghton / Seymour Lawrence, 1990. A series of interconnected stories about a platoon of soldiers during the Vietnam War. These stories depict events and contain language that may be disturbing to readers. **(challenge)**

Remarque, Erich Maria. *All Quiet on the Western Front.* New York: Harcourt, 1945. A riveting antiwar novel about World War I, as told from a young German soldier's perspective. **(average)**

NONFICTION

Detzer, John. *An Asian Tragedy: America and Vietnam.* Connecticut: Millbrook, 1992. A comprehensive analysis of the Vietnam War, filled with interesting facts and anecdotes. **(easy)**

Edelman, Bernard, ed. *Dear America: Letters Home from Vietnam.* New York: Norton, 1985. A moving collection of letters written by soldiers serving in Vietnam. **(average)**

Fitzgerald, Frances. *Fire in the Lake: The Vietnamese and the Americans in Vietnam.* New York: Random, 1972. A thoughtful, in-depth examination of U.S. military intervention in Vietnam in relation to Vietnamese culture and history. Won the Pulitzer Prize, National Book Award, and other prestigious honors. **(challenge)**

Karnow, Stanley. *Vietnam: The War Nobody Won.* New York: Foreign Aid Policy Association, 1983. A concise account of U.S. military involvement in Vietnam and its impact. **(average)**

Reinberg, Linda. *In the Field: The Language of the Vietnam War.* New York: Facts on File, 1991. A fascinating dictionary containing almost 5,000 entries of slang expressions, military jargon, acronyms, and technical words from the Vietnam War. **(average)**

MULTIMEDIA

All Quiet on the Western Front. Dir. Lewis Milestone. Perf. Lew Ayres, Louis Wolheim. Videocasette. Universal: MCA Home Video. 130 min. Academy award-winning 1930 film based on Erich Remarque's compelling antiwar novel. **(videocassette)**

Beyond the Wall: Stories Behind the Vietnam Memorial. CD-ROM. Magnet Interactive, 1995. A chronicle of the aftermath of the Vietnam War and the evolution of the Vietnam Veterans Memorial. **(CD-ROM)**

Dear America: Letters Home from Vietnam. Video Recording. HBO, 1988. 84 min. Readings by Sean Penn, Robin Williams, and Robert DeNiro. Note: The film contains some brief scenes of nudity. **(videocassette)**

No Time for Tears: Vietnam—The Women Who Served. Video Recording. West End Films, 1993. Videocassette recording. 59 minutes. A documentary filled with personal accounts of women Vietnam veterans—nurse, doctors, and teachers. **(videocassette)**

Vietnam—The Dream Shot Down: In the Land of Jim Crow. Video recording. 23 minutes. A hard-hitting documentary about African-American soldiers in the Vietnam War. Note: The film contains strong language that might be disturbing to some viewers. **(videocassette)**